OVERCOMING SPIRITUAL
DISCOURAGEMENT

TIMOTHY M. GALLAGHER, O.M.V.

OVERCOMING
SPIRITUAL
DISCOURAGEMENT

The Wisdom and Spiritual Power
of Venerable Bruno Lanteri

EWTN PUBLISHING, INC.
IRONDALE, ALABAMA

Imprimi potest: Fr. James A. Walther, O.M.V.,
Provincial of the Province of St. Ignatius
July 29, 2019

EWTN Publishing, Inc.
5817 Old Leeds Road, Irondale, AL 35210

Distributed by Sophia Institute Press, Box 5284, Manchester, NH 03108.

ISBN 978-1-68278-095-4

Library of Congress Control Number:2019948535

From the Decree of St. Paul VI Declaring the Heroicity of the Virtues of Venerable Bruno Lanteri:

His Holiness, Paul VI, having prayed earnestly, in conclusion, on this day, after celebrating Mass with great fervor, called the Most Reverend Cardinals Arcadio Maria Larraona, Prefect of the Sacred Congregation of Rites; Benedetto Aloisi Masella, Relator of the Cause; and me with them, as Secretary, and solemnly decreed that "the Servant of God, Pio Brunone Lanteri, priest and founder of the Congregation of the Oblates of the Virgin Mary, practiced the theological virtues of faith, hope, and charity toward God and neighbor, as also the cardinal virtues of prudence, justice, temperance, and fortitude, with their associated virtues, to a heroic degree."

Rome, 23 November 1965

Arcadio Card. M. Larraona,
Prefect of the Sacred Congregation of Rites

Ferdinando Antonelli, O.F.M., Secretary

CONTENTS

Introduction 1

Prologue: A Personal Word 3

1. Living with Hope 11

2. Living the Spiritual Life 35

3. Living the Day with Jesus 55

4. Living the Cross and Resurrection of Jesus 69

5. Living with Mary 85

6. Living with Courage 93

A Final Word 109

Prayer for the Intercession of Venerable Bruno 111

Resources 113

Sources 115

About the Author 119

INTRODUCTION

Who of us does not struggle at times, perhaps often, with discouragement in our spiritual lives? Who of us cannot benefit from help in overcoming such discouragement?

Six years ago, I published a biography of Venerable Bruno, *Begin Again: The Life and Spiritual Legacy of Bruno Lanteri*. This full-length book guides the reader through the life and teaching of Venerable Bruno. The present book focuses on a single theme in Venerable Bruno's spiritual teaching, that expressed in the title: *Overcoming Spiritual Discouragement*. Its 114 quotations offer you direct access to Venerable Bruno's spiritual advice to the many who, in times of discouragement, sought his help.

I have chosen these quotations from his letters of spiritual direction, primarily those to laypeople, both men and women, from his personal spiritual notes, and from programs for the spiritual life composed for himself or others. Each quotation, with its individual nuances, offers encouragement and hope to people who need to hear this message. Venerable Bruno's counsels are timeless, and they speak to our hearts today as they did to the hearts of those who first received them.

I present these quotations according to six chapters, corresponding to various emphases in Venerable Bruno's teaching: a call to hope, practical advice for the life of prayer, how to live the day with

Jesus, solace in time of suffering, the blessing of Mary's presence, and thoughts that build courage.

Each quotation offers a counsel, a proposal, or a teaching. Always, as you will see, Venerable Bruno remains concrete and practical; his focus is living the spiritual life. To each quotation, I have appended a personal commentary. These are generally unstudied, from the heart, spontaneous, born of long association with these texts and the one who wrote them. My commentary seeks less to add than to explicate and to slow the pace, so that the reader may enter more deeply into the thoughts Venerable Bruno wishes to convey.

All translations are the author's. For those who wish to pursue them, I provide the source of each quotation at the conclusion of this book.

How should this book be read? That is your choice! Many, I believe, will find that a slow pace works best, perhaps one or two quotations at a time. Some may benefit from a more continuous reading. Others may wish to mingle these approaches. I believe that a return, perhaps several times, to the texts that most speak to your heart will repay the effort.

May this book be for you a source of hope and encouragement!

Prologue

A PERSONAL WORD

I first learned of Venerable Bruno when I encountered the Oblates of the Virgin Mary. I knew that I was called to the priesthood but did not yet know where. I had visited my diocesan seminary and a number of religious communities, but nothing had seemed the right fit.

Then my mother found an article about the Oblates and showed it to me. I was immediately intrigued. The Marian component of the Oblates' spirituality spoke to me, as did the community's warm support of papal teaching and its emphasis on prayer. It seemed to have a clear and compelling identity. It was then that I first read about Venerable Bruno, though he remained in the background as I focused more on the present-day Oblate community in my discernment. I visited with one of the Oblate priests and, the next fall, entered the community in its house just outside of Rome.

Then followed something that, I believe, only God's grace can explain. Venerable Bruno quickly began to draw me in a powerful way. I say that grace alone can explain this because I have only experienced this kind of spiritual attraction twice in my life: toward Venerable Bruno and, later and very much related, toward the Spiritual Exercises of St. Ignatius that Venerable Bruno so loved.

I studied Italian and still remember the first book I read, not without struggle, in the new language: a popular 1950 biography of

Venerable Bruno by Icilio Felici, the full title of which, in translation, reads, *A Standard Never Laid Down: Pio Bruno Lanteri, Founder of the Oblates of the Virgin Mary and Precursor of the Catholic Action Movement.* It was exciting to read in a new language, and it was my first substantial introduction to Venerable Bruno. This only whetted my appetite for more.

Not long after, I found in the community's library the massive thousand-page volume prepared for Venerable Bruno's cause for canonization, compiled by Monsignor Amato Frutaz in 1945. It contained documents from Venerable Bruno's life and writings in the three languages that he spoke and in which he wrote: Italian, French, and Latin. Monsignor Frutaz's commentary was in Latin.

I was delighted to find that I could read the Italian documents, and I knew immediately that I must learn French and Latin so that I could assimilate the rest. In the next years, I acquired a reading knowledge of both. Later, when I realized that German, too, would be needed to read texts concerning Venerable Bruno, I studied that language as well.

In all this was an interest, a pull, a something — I would say, a grace — that removed any difficulty or struggle I might otherwise have felt. I simply wanted full access to Venerable Bruno, and I wanted it from the heart. It would have been harder *not* to pursue getting to know him.

During my seminary studies, as often as possible I chose essay topics related to Venerable Bruno. Among these was a study of *The Journey of the Mind to God* by St. Bonaventure, a favorite of Venerable Bruno, and a reflection on a work he wrote in defense of the teaching of St. Alphonsus Liguori, another saint Venerable Bruno esteemed highly. Gradually, I was growing acquainted with the sources and expanding my knowledge of Venerable Bruno. The sense of attraction only deepened.

Vatican II had asked that religious communities renew themselves according to "their founders' spirit and special aims" (*Decree*

A Personal Word

on the Renewal and Adaptation of Religious Life, 2). During these years, in keeping with the Council's directive, Oblate Father Paolo Calliari published Venerable Bruno's letters in five volumes, and then a substantial biography in five further volumes. The Oblates in Rome also began an in-house publication of Venerable Bruno's writings. New material in abundance was now available in printed form.

In the year before my ordination and in the years following, I did graduate studies in spiritual theology at the Pontifical Gregorian University. Among my professors was Jesuit Manuel Ruiz Jurado, to whom I will be forever grateful. As I will tell later in this book, a remark of his regarding Venerable Bruno's interest in the Spiritual Exercises of St. Ignatius shaped much of my studies in these years. I asked him to serve as moderator for my licentiate (the ecclesiastical equivalent of a master's degree) thesis on this topic. The months spent in writing this thesis led me further into Venerable Bruno's life and thought.

I then undertook a doctoral thesis, again under Father Ruiz Jurado, in which I explored the place of the Spiritual Exercises in Venerable Bruno's life and charism as founder. For two years, I did little else than read and ponder the writings of my community's founder, and I was blessed to do so with the original documents conserved in the Oblates' archive. This was a unique opportunity for which I have always been grateful: There was no mediation, no secondary author between me and Venerable Bruno. I was holding, reading, and examining the very paper on which he wrote. I could see his corrections as he sought the precise word he wanted and the additions he made as he reflected further on the topic.

Living in Italy during these years also helped greatly in coming to know Venerable Bruno. I spent twelve years in that country and learned the language, culture, history, and literature. I read the memoirs of figures important in Venerable Bruno's life and explored the Church history of his time. Repeated trips to his own region of Piedmont, the northwestern province of present-day Italy, familiarized me with the topography, cities and towns, landscapes, and culture of the area. When Father Calliari, who had such deep knowledge of Venerable Bruno, offered a tour of the places of his life in Piedmont and France, I was delighted. For two weeks, we traveled daily in Fr. Calliari's battered Volkswagen, visiting place after place. I still have the notes and photos from that trip.

When my studies finished, the superior sent me to our seminary residence in Boston where I taught for five years. Each year, I gave talks to our novices about the life and spirituality of Venerable Bruno, as well as the history of his era. Later these talks were videotaped as a series of thirty-eight conferences. When, after those years, I was named novice master, such teaching continued.

Time passed, and my Oblate ministry led me to publish a series of books on Ignatian themes. Then, one day, our provincial asked me to write a biography of Venerable Bruno. My "yes" was both a response to religious authority and to a desire I had long felt. It was a daunting task! The biography required five years — three of additional study and two of writing. During these years, I lived in Venerable Bruno's world, his culture, his times, and his concerns. That immersion decisively changed my understanding of him.

Before then, I had seen the dedication, the single-mindedness, and the heroism. Now I also saw the struggles, the disappointments, the physical burdens, the pain of loss — that is, I saw Venerable Bruno's human side. I had long admired his strength, but it was his weakness that finally won me completely to him. He knew our struggles — my struggles, too; he was not spared them. And he did not succumb to them. He gave me, as he had to so many in his life, hope and encouragement. For this reason, at the editor's suggestion, I titled the book *Begin Again: The Life and Spiritual Legacy of Bruno Lanteri*. This was central to his message: Never give in to discouragement; lift your heart immediately to the God who so loves you; and begin again, always, day after day, if necessary even hour after hour. Venerable Bruno endlessly repeated such counsel.

One day, as I was writing the final chapters of *Begin Again*, I put down the pen and sat at my desk. For a time, I remained seated, simply absorbing the content I was describing. Because Venerable Bruno lived in community during his last three years, we have abundant witness to his life during them. Having explored anecdote after anecdote of warm, rich, holiness, I found myself saying, "This man is a saint. He lived with heroic virtue. Before, I knew this because the Church has formally proclaimed it. Now I know it myself. This man must be canonized!" Since then, I have done what I can to bring his life and teaching to others, convinced that he has an important message for our times, increasingly similar to his own.

While I was writing *Begin Again*, my father died. Now my mother was alone and needed the presence of her family. I spent time in a local parish, helping with Masses and confessions, writing, and assisting my mother. At the same time, my speaking engagements increased. The combined pressure led to a growth on a vocal cord and the near loss of my voice. I had to suspend all ministry. When medication failed to resolve the problem, the doctor performed vocal surgery. Complications led to a second surgery two weeks later. Over the next several years, four more vocal surgeries followed, each one accompanied by a temporary loss of my voice. As this cycle repeated again and again, I grew discouraged. I wondered if I would ever return to normal life and ministry.

Then, three years after that first surgery—I wish this had not taken me three years!—it occurred to me to pray to Venerable Bruno daily, asking for the voice I needed. At the start of each day, I said the prayer for his intercession found at the end of this book. And things started to happen.

On one trip, I needed a refill of a medication that I was taking for another issue. The refill was lost in the mail, and so for some weeks I went without it. I found that my voice improved. On another occasion, a doctor suggested a change in diet, again for another matter. I made the change, and once again found that my voice improved. As such occurrences multiplied, I could not but see the hand of Venerable Bruno in response to this daily prayer.

That was six years ago. I still say that prayer daily. Since I began praying it, I have needed no further surgeries. As you can imagine, I will say that prayer every day until I die. With the years, I have added the needs of others to that daily prayer.

On a lesser note, knowing Venerable Bruno's love for reading, I have long asked his help when I need to find the right book for a given occasion. This prayer, too, I consistently find answered.

Since writing the biography, I have begun speaking on the life and message of Venerable Bruno. The response has shown me in a further and more powerful way the richness of his witness and teaching. As you will see in this book, his counsel is warm, understanding, ever encouraging, ever a source of new hope. His practical advice about the spiritual life leads people to say, quite simply, "That's doable!" And in difficult times, when discouragement may readily surface, his firm call to trust and confidence resonates more and more deeply. In a way I could not have foreseen years ago, his message grows increasingly contemporary.

Bruno Lanteri was born in northern Italy in 1759 and died there in 1830. These were the tumultuous years in which the French Revolution convulsed first France and then all of Europe. War, political subjection, and persecution of the Church followed in Venerable Bruno's region of Piedmont. In these same years, the Church struggled to free itself from a grim Jansenism—a teaching that portrayed God as an easily-angered judge, and that led people to fear rather than love him—and the burdensome pastoral practice it imposed. Ever in the thick of events and quick to perceive and meet the Church's needs, all the while battling severe physical problems, through seventy-one years of life and forty-eight of priesthood, Venerable Bruno brought hope, solace, encouragement, new vigor of faith, and apostolic energy to countless men and women. The selections of his writings presented in this book will reveal why this was so.

May his words open to you that same path to hope.

Venerable Bruno Lanteri

Chapter One

LIVING WITH HOPE

1. *Say then with boldness, "Now I begin," and go forward constantly in God's service. Do not look back so often, because one who looks back cannot run. And do not be content to begin only for this year. Begin every day, because it is for every day, even for every hour of the day, that the Lord taught us to say in the Our Father, "Forgive us our trespasses," and, "Give us this day our daily bread."*

In any time of discouragement, when you feel that you have failed yet again, that there are irreversible consequences, that it is too late, that you will never change, say, "Now I begin!" And say it with boldness—boldness because God's grace is always with you, because he loves you, because it is never too late, because nothing is impossible for God (Luke 1:37). There is nothing you can ever have done, nowhere you can ever have been in your life that can ever stop you from turning right now to God, asking forgiveness if you need it—a forgiveness that God delights to give, rejoices to give, is eager to give (Luke 15)—and beginning again. I have seen this counsel of Venerable Bruno give hope to many.

"Do not look back so often, because one who looks back cannot run." Try this! Try to run while looking back over your shoulder. You will quickly laugh and give it up—or fall over! Do not allow your heart to dwell so often on your past failings. It is more important and more blessed to begin now, to look forward, to follow where God is leading now.

Do this not once a year, not even at the start of every day—both wonderful practices—but even every hour of the day, with hope and trust in God's love. Can you try this? Can you see the difference this will make? The hope this will bring? The courage you will feel to fulfill the tasks God has given you? Then forgiveness and daily bread, the daily nourishment we need for our bodily and spiritual lives, will gently and joyfully enter our hearts.

> 2. *Be on guard against discouragement and lack of trust. Strive to do well all that you do, but do this with respect for your humanity, without striving for an impossible perfection, focusing simply on the day at hand. Remember that "the just man falls seven times a day," and so you will find blessing in beginning not only every day, but every hour.*

The great obstacle in the spiritual life is discouragement. For those who love the Lord and sincerely try, with all their failings, to follow him, this is the great danger. And so Venerable Bruno begins here: "Be on guard against discouragement!" Are you discouraged these days? This day? Be aware and watchful against this feeling. Venerable Bruno will suggest concrete ways to combat discouragement, as we will see.

Yes, strive to do well all that you do—your prayer, your work, your relationships, your service to others, your life in the Church—but do it with respect for your humanity. If you find yourself straining to get that last good task done in the face of utter exhaustion; if you find yourself taking on one more responsibility when you know that you are already too stressed; if you consider undertaking a further spiritual practice that you know will only be possible when nothing unforeseen interferes—and you know that unforeseen things will occur—know that God is not asking this of you right now. Yes, strive to do well all that you do. God does want this of you. But God also wants you to respect the humanity he has given you, the humanity that he himself took on and that he loves.

Nor does God ask you to strive for an impossible perfection. Rather, focus simply on the day at hand. Do what God has given you to do today. That is enough. That is your path to holiness; it is all you need.

I have come to love the biblical affirmation that the just man falls seven times a day (Prov. 24:16). We do! That is why we have a penitential rite at the start of every Mass: "I confess ... that I have greatly sinned." That is why Night Prayer in the Liturgy of the Hours begins with an examination of conscience. That is why we have the Sacrament of Reconciliation. Our failings should neither surprise us nor discourage us. Here, too, Venerable Bruno encourages us to begin again—and not only every day, but every hour.

Reread these words of Venerable Bruno slowly.

3. *Keep far from you the spirit of sadness and melancholy. Show yourself joyful even when you do not feel so because of physical problems. At such times more than ever, guard against closing in on yourself, and turn your thoughts to Paradise, because it is yours.*

Avoid sadness; avoid melancholy. These weigh on you and on others around you. Then this remarkable counsel: "Show yourself joyful even when you do not feel so because of physical problems." So many of us know the burden of physical maladies, pains, limitations. We know how physical pain especially diverts our attention, how hard it is to ignore, how easy it is to become wrapped in it. Show yourself joyful in such times, says Venerable Bruno, even when you feel frustrated or angry or miserable. This is not easy:

We need God's help to do this. But people around us will love us for it and will take strength from us in their own pain.

As mentioned, some years ago, I underwent a series of surgeries, and life became difficult. I took this saying of Venerable Bruno, printed it, and taped it on the wall of my room where I would see it often in the day: "Show yourself joyful even when you do not feel so because of physical problems." It was a great help to me.

At such times, do not close in on yourself, but remain open to others. Think of heaven, of paradise, of the meaning of your pain; it is neither empty nor simply a cruel fate, but a preparation for an eternal reward. "I consider that the sufferings of this present time are as nothing compared with the glory to be revealed for us" (Rom. 8:18).

4. *We should always keep in our hearts this saying of the Holy Spirit:* Sentite de Deo in bonitate *[Think of God in a spirit of goodness: see Wis. 1:1]. And so we should seek sentiments worthy of God first in ourselves so as then to inspire them in others, and attain the goal of loving him and bringing all to love him.*

Sentite de Deo in bonitate. This verse from Scripture was a leit-motif for Venerable Bruno, repeated over and over again. Are you afraid of God? Do you follow him with faith and love but also with a burden in your heart? Are there gray areas on the margins of your heart, places where you feel, with sadness, that God is disappointed with you, that he would wish to see you make more progress, overcome that defect more firmly, cease to fail in that area? *Sentite de Deo in bonitate!* Think of God in a spirit of goodness! Let your heart expand in knowing his understanding, his eagerness to forgive and to heal, the delight he takes in you, and, simply, his goodness. Yes, *Sentite de Deo in bonitate* — and share these sentiments with others.

Here is a young girl who has acted out at school. She has done something seriously wrong, not a small or light thing. Word has reached her father, and he awaits her at home. She reaches home and stands outside the front door, hesitating. She knows that her father is within. She is afraid. She opens the door, and there is her father. He does not say a word. He approaches her, embraces her, and says, "I love you." Now she can tell him everything.

Think of God in a spirit of goodness, in a way worthy of who God truly is. As we do, we will grow in love of him and bring others to love him as well.

5. *Keep constantly before you these two proposals that I urge you to renew often and with a holy persistence: first, never to offend God knowingly, and, second, if you should fall, never to persevere in this with your will, but, with humility and courage, to rise immediately and begin again, firmly convinced that God forgives you in the instant itself that with humility and trust you ask his forgiveness.*

A holy persistence. We will see Venerable Bruno return to this often. Here he encourages a holy persistence in two things. We will fail out of weakness, out of tiredness, out of a failure to understand a situation, and for similar reasons. This is our human condition. But try with a holy persistence never to offend God knowingly, with your eyes open.

Yet if you do fail, never remain in this situation, never let your will persist in this. On the contrary, with humility—a blessed virtue that draws God's grace upon you—and courage, rise immediately and (once more this counsel) begin again. This "immediately" is another refrain in Venerable Bruno's spiritual guidance. Do not remain in the situation of failure! Rise immediately, now, without delay, and begin again. These two proposals, practiced with a holy persistence, will close the door to discouragement and open it to joy.

Venerable Bruno knows his correspondent, knows that she sincerely loves the Lord and tries her best to serve him, and that she, like us, has her failings—failings in the ongoing actions and interactions of daily life. Thus he can confidently counsel her to be "firmly convinced that God forgives you in the instant itself that with humility and trust you ask his forgiveness." In the instant itself. I have seen this teaching lift the hearts of dedicated people long burdened by a sense of their failings. Can you let Venerable Bruno say these words to you as well?

6. *It is very important that we understand deeply how good God is and not measure him by our own limitations or think that he tires of our wavering, weakness, and negligence. Our God is not such. Let us think of him as he truly is, filled with goodness, mercy, and compassion, and let us know him as the loving Father he is, who raises us when we have fallen, who never tires of forgiving us, and to whom we give great joy and honor when we seek forgiveness.*

"*It is very important!*" What has such importance? That we understand deeply how good God is and that "we not measure him by our own limitations." It is so easy for us to do this, to measure God by our own limitations and so to think that "he tires of our wavering, weakness, and negligence."

Here is a person who is always late. Here is another who promises to help but seldom does. Here is another who often leaves undone work that we need for our projects. Here is another who hesitates, wavers, and never comes to a decision. How quickly we tire of this! And so readily we think that God is like this with us—that he tires of our hesitations, our weaknesses, and our failures to fulfill our commitments in prayer, in love of others, and in service. It is *very important* that we not measure God by our own limitations.

This counsel has come to mean much for me over years. It has made me realize how easily I do just what Venerable Bruno so strongly urges us to avoid: measure God by our own limitations. I love the freedom to which this wisdom leads.

"Our God is not such," is not limited according to our human limitations. Think of him, then, Bruno says, as he truly is, filled with goodness, mercy, compassion—"as the loving Father he is." "Father" for Venerable Bruno is a warm, rich, loving word. He lost his mother when he was four years old and was raised by his father, a skilled doctor, a dedicated Catholic, and a good father to whom Bruno was always grateful. Further, his spiritual father for twenty years, Fr. Diessbach, was a holy and wise man, to whom Bruno was likewise grateful and through whom he found his spiritual identity. "Father" for Bruno evokes the image of a loving Father, who raises us when we have fallen, who never tires of forgiving, and who feels great joy—not just joy, but great joy—and is honored when we ask his forgiveness.

Bruno will return to this theme, too, repeatedly: If we can grasp who our God truly is, the loving Father that he truly is, burdens will lift from our hearts and we will grow in the spiritual life—because we will know that we are loved. St. Paul VI describes "the secret of the unfathomable joy that dwells in Jesus" and explains, "If Jesus radiates such peace, such assurance, such happiness, such availability, it is because of the inexpressible love by which he knows that he is loved by his Father" (*Apostolic Exhortation On Christian Joy*). We have the same loving Father.

> 7. *I urge you to begin each day leaving the past to the mercy of the Lord, and the future to his Divine Providence. Do not let yourself be troubled by anything, not even by your own failings, taking care to overcome them immediately by an act of love of God.*

Begin your spiritual journey anew each day. What will help you do this is to leave the past — any failings, sins, weaknesses, and failures — to God's mercy, the best hands in which you can leave them, and the future to his Divine Providence, again the best hands in which you can leave it. In this way, both worries about the past and concerns for the future slip from our shoulders, and we are the more ready to begin again today, in this present moment that God gives us.

"Do not let yourself be troubled by anything, not even by your own failings." By anything. Not even your own failings. Often, it is precisely our own failings that most trouble us. "I wish that I were stronger, more patient, more constant, less wavering, less prone to fall, less overwhelmed by discouragement."

This was the experience of Peter after the catch of fish (Luke 5:1-11), when through this sign he realized that the divine had come close to him in Jesus. There in the boat, filled almost to sinking with fish, he fell on his knees before Jesus and said, "Depart from me, for I am a sinful man, O Lord." In other words: "I can't be this close to you. I am a sinner, a sinful man. Let there be more distance between us." I have always loved Jesus's response. He does not argue with Peter. He simply says the words that Peter most needs to hear, "Do not be afraid," and confirms Peter's belonging to his mission. "Do not let yourself be troubled by anything, not even by your own failings."

Rather, "take care to overcome them immediately by an act of love of God." Once again, that word, "immediately." Do not hesitate. Do not wait. When you see your failings, simply turn your heart to God and express your love for him. And these failings will be overcome.

8. *If I should fall a thousand times a day, a thousand times a day I will begin again, with new awareness of my weakness,*

promising God, with a peaceful heart, to amend my life. I
will never think of God as if he were of our condition and
grows weary of our wavering, weakness, and negligence.
Rather, I will think of what is truly characteristic of him and
what he prizes most highly, that is, his goodness and mercy,
knowing that he is a loving Father who understands our
weakness, is patient with us, and forgives us.

"If I should fall a thousand times a day, a thousand times a day I will begin again." A thousand times a day: I lost my patience this morning at breakfast, again and again at work, this evening with my spouse, my children, my parishioners, my brothers in community, my sisters in community, the others in the group.... Even a thousand times a day. Then, a thousand times a day I will begin again.

Bruno wrote these words in a personal spiritual program when he was twenty-two years old, and offered them often to others in spiritual direction. This is among his most characteristic sayings.

Stop here for a moment. Reread these words: "If I should fall a thousand times a day, a thousand times a day I will begin again." Think about them. Pray about them for a moment. Do they apply to your heart, your life? Ask the Lord for this courage and this hope.

9. *Heroic hope. He held well impressed in his heart and ever*
present to him the maxim that "the one who hopes for every-
thing, obtains everything." If he sensed that anyone weak-
ened in hope, he corrected him with ardor and encouraged
him to renew his practice of this virtue, in which, because
it is a theological virtue, there can be no excess. He would
say with energy that just as we cannot believe too much in
God nor love God too much, so also we cannot hope too
much in God. And in saying this, we saw him deeply moved

OVERCOMING SPIRITUAL DISCOURAGEMENT

by the great ardor and liveliness of his zeal. (Witness of a priest close to Venerable Bruno for twenty years)

"Well-impressed," "ever-present," "ardor," "encouragement," "energy," "deeply moved," "great ardor," "great liveliness," "zeal": Venerable Bruno, from his heart, with energy and warmth, repeatedly, and at the first sign of weakening, encourages us to place our hope in God. As Bruno looked at his world and at the members of the Church around him, he saw plainly how easily people can lose hope. Is that less true today? What do we feel as we read the daily news? What stirs in our hearts as we watch the sufferings of our Church? We can never hope too much: "The one who hopes for everything—everything!—obtains everything."

St. John Paul II was asked how he could repeat to the people of this world, with all the sad and tragic events they witness, "Be not afraid." He answered, "Why should we have no fear? Because man has been redeemed by God.... In the Redemption we find the most profound basis for the words 'Be not afraid!': 'For God so loved the world that he gave his only Son' (John 3:16). This Son is always present in the history of humanity as Redeemer. The Redemption pervades all of human history."

Then the Holy Father gave us words that I return to more than any others he wrote or spoke: "The power of Christ's Cross and Resurrection is greater than any evil man could or should fear." I love the truth, the realism, and the confidence of these words. There are evils in this world that we can and that we should fear. But there is also a power in this world, a power that pervades all of human history, today as well, greater than any of them—the power of Christ's Cross and Resurrection, that is, the power of the Redemption. And so the Holy Father concludes, "It is very important to cross the threshold of hope, not to stop before it, but to let oneself be led" (*Crossing the Threshold of Hope*, 219, 223–224).

We can never hope too much. The one who hopes for everything, obtains everything.

10. *Let us learn to go forward even in the midst of our faults, and never to stop because of them. If we do not know well this art, which is not at all easy for us, we risk turning back. We must presuppose that we will commit faults, because only in heaven is it given to serve God without them. Whence we must learn to fall, yes, but to rise immediately, and to seek forgiveness without being surprised or burdened by regret. We must not give up, no matter how many or how great the failings may be, but rather humble ourselves, repent, and rise from them the more distanced from them, if we have the courage for this, because this is great wisdom and an excellent means for making progress.*

Once again: "Whence we must learn to fall, yes, but to lift ourselves up *immediately*." The serenity of this affirmation speaks to me: we must presuppose that we will commit many faults. Our prayer will not be what we would have wished, but too little, too distracted. Or we will be more self-centered today than we would want—less patient, less willing to help, to listen, to encourage, more self-indulgent than we hoped.... Our call is to rise *immediately* and peacefully to ask God's forgiveness, without being surprised by our stumbling, without allowing regret to burden us. On the contrary, we rise from these failings humbler, less attached to them, and closer to God. Without this "art" we run the risk of losing heart and pulling back; but with it, we go confidently toward God. Have you learned this art? Can you learn it? Ask God, the loving Father that Venerable Bruno knew him to be, to teach you this response to your failings.

11. *Holiness does not consist in never failing, but in rising immediately, recognizing our weakness and asking God's*

forgiveness, and in doing this with peace of heart, without letting ourselves be troubled.

Holiness itself consists in this grace-filled "art." Do we have this understanding of holiness? If we do, does not holiness immediately become more accessible to us? Does it not become evident that the universal call to holiness (as identified by the Second Vatican Council) is not a remote ideal but real for all of us? Holiness does not consist in rising above all failings so that we never fail; it consists in failing, and in fact, repeatedly, but each time rising quickly and asking God's forgiveness, all the while maintaining our peace of heart. Our failings need never close the doors of our hearts to God. If we respond to them in the way Venerable Bruno proposes, these very failings are transformed into stepping-stones to holiness. Can you not try to live this way?

12. *Your affliction in regard to the past has no basis; it is simply a temptation of the enemy. I assure you of this in the name of God. Instead, therefore, of giving in to this, give glory to God and thank him from your heart for the infinite goodness with which he has forgiven everything. This same enemy does not stop at attacking you only with regard to the past; he seeks to attack you regarding the future as well. Be watchful of this. If you did not make all the progress you wished in the past year, such will not be the case this year if you humble yourself and have all the greater hope in God, asking him without ceasing to grant you these two graces that we need so much and that he so desires to give you, having promised this to you and merited it for you.*

Does your past burden you? Do your failings and sins of the past weigh on you? Do they make it hard to believe — really believe, deep down, from the heart — that God loves you? Be sure that this is not the voice of God! Our enemy willingly works in our vulnerabilities, causing this sense of burden. You have brought all this to God in the past and asked his forgiveness. Instead, therefore, of letting your heart be afflicted, thank God from your heart for the infinite goodness with which he has forgiven you everything.

This same enemy, Venerable Bruno continues, will also try to afflict you regarding the future: "Look at you! Look at how little progress you made this last year, in the last years, in past months. Why do you think it will be any different now, this year? You will never make any real progress." Venerable Bruno urges us to be watchful of this! These voices also are not of God, but clearly of the enemy. We need only two gifts of grace: a humble heart and one filled with ever greater hope in God. Ask God for these two gifts today. Right now. God greatly desires to give both to us. Jesus, on the Cross, merited them for us.

> 13. *Do you not yet see that the enemy seeks in this way to strip you of your peace and confidence in God, two dispositions we so need in order to pray well? Follow, therefore, the counsel of Saint Teresa: "Let nothing disturb you," not even your own failings, because these are the object and the foundation of the infinite mercy of God that infinitely surpasses the malice of all the sins of the world. Firmly resolved never to let yourself be troubled by anything in the world, present yourself humbly and with full confidence to the Lord in prayer, and he will not fail to have compassion on you.*

God and the enemy — two contrasting approaches. The enemy seeks to strip you of your peace, to weaken your confidence in God, to burden you, to discourage you. Have you felt this? This is not God's voice. God speaks to your heart: "Let nothing disturb you, not even your own failings. My infinite mercy envelops and heals them. Do not let yourself be troubled. Come with an open, sincere, humble heart before me, with great confidence, in prayer, and be sure of the warm compassion of my heart."

14. *Do not be concerned if prayer does not go as you would wish; it is enough that it be as God wishes. And this is not difficult; you need only avoid voluntary negligence.*

You give time to prayer, but it is difficult, dry, different from what you wish it to be. Yes, learn from our rich Catholic spiritual tradition how to pray: the Liturgy of the Hours, *lectio divina*, Ignatian reflective meditation or imaginative contemplation, the Rosary—whatever best helps you to pray. If you have questions and access to a wise and competent spiritual advisor or to helpful reading or digital resources, then seek answers. But when you have done what you can, and still your prayer does not go as you wish, do not be troubled. It is enough, Venerable Bruno says, that it go as God wishes. And this, he continues, is not difficult. All we need do is avoid voluntary negligence in preparing, in giving time, in finding a suitable place, and in peacefully seeking to be attentive in the prayer itself. We can all do this.

One of the most helpful counsels regarding prayer I have found is from St. Teresa of Avila. After the wealth of teaching she gives on prayer, St. Teresa says that, in the end, having a growing prayer life depends on one thing: fidelity. Just never give up. No matter how difficult, empty, fruitless, or imperfect your prayer may seem, just never stop praying, and your prayer life will grow. I have witnessed the truth of this saying often over the years, and it gives me courage when prayer is difficult. Do not be concerned if prayer does not go as you wish; it is enough that it be as God wishes. And this is not difficult; you need only avoid any intentional neglect in prayer.

15. Do not be surprised to find yourself spiritually dry. This is a human condition to which we are subject, and you will profit spiritually by it when you bear it with patience and perseverance, striving to avoid voluntary negligence. And if you fall into voluntary negligences, profit from these by humbling yourself before God, and renew the resolve always to begin again.

At times you will not feel God's closeness, and prayer itself will be dry. You will wish for more energy, more zeal, more enthusiasm in spiritual things. You may feel sadness that today, this week, this month, prayer seems so dry, so spiritually arid. Do not be surprised to find yourself dry. This, Venerable Bruno affirms, is a human condition, a condition to which we are subject at times because of this body-soul composite that is our human reality. Physical indisposition or emotional weariness play their part. We profit spiritually when we bear this condition with patience and perseverance, striving to avoid any voluntary—freely chosen—negligence. Even should we fall into this, we benefit spiritually when we present ourselves humbly before God and begin again. When prayer is dry, do your best, and never allow yourself to be discouraged.

16. If you wish to recognize the enemy, even when he presents himself under the appearance of good, note whether what he proposes causes discouragement when he proposes it, because this is a sure sign of a hidden temptation.

A thought comes. This is something I could do. It would be good; it would help me grow, serve better, respond more fully to the Lord. Is it of God? Is there a temptation hidden in it? Look into your heart. What does this thought stir there? If it is discouragement, this thought is not of God. "The fruit of the Spirit is love, joy, peace, patience, kindness, generosity, faithfulness, gentleness, self-control" (Gal. 5:22–23).

17. *Be of good heart, because the Lord is with you, and he loves you.*

These are words from a letter that Venerable Bruno wrote to a dedicated woman who was often discouraged. She copied them and kept them, even after Venerable Bruno's death. They clearly meant much to her.

Read them slowly. Again.

For years now, I have taped these words on the door of the office where I meet people for spiritual direction. I want people, with whatever burdens they may carry, to receive these words as the first message and one that sets the tone for the sharing to follow. Perhaps I do this also because they speak to my heart, and I, too, want to see them often.

18. *I find that you are always the same, that is, that you easily fall into discouragement, and this is your principal defect, which, if you give into it, will cause you many others. Therefore, it is here more than anywhere else that you must strengthen yourself by proposing always to desire to be invincible in hope, whatever may happen, and however weak you see yourself to be; because for our part, the basis of our hope is precisely our weakness, and on God's part, his mercy, which is nothing other than a heartfelt compassion for our weakness.*

Over and over, Venerable Bruno returns to this: Discouragement is the main obstacle in our spiritual lives. The main obstacle is not our more obvious failings—our impatience, our slowness to help others, our limitations in prayer, our self-indulgence, our failures to listen. The great obstacle is giving in to discouragement when we see such failings in ourselves.

Of course the enemy wants this! Such discouragement, as Venerable Bruno affirms, if we give in to it, will lead to further spiritual problems.

Therefore, "it is here"—when you see your failures—"more than anywhere else," that you must "propose always to desire to be invincible in hope, whatever may happen, and however weak you see yourself to be." "Whatever may happen"—today's failings, last week's; "and however weak you see yourself to be"—the same failings, the same sense that you simply cannot overcome them. *Right here*, you must be invincible in hope.

You answer, "I hear that counsel, and I love it. But I do not feel invincible in hope. So often I feel just the contrary." Venerable Bruno replies, "Yes, but can you renew this proposal of hope? Can you ask God's help to embrace it? Can you remember that, 'for our part, the basis of our hope is precisely our weakness' and that, on God's part, the basis of our hope is 'his mercy, which is nothing other than a heartfelt compassion for our weakness?'" When we open our weakness to the heartfelt compassion God has for that weakness, discouragement wanes, and hope grows.

> 19. *I recommend that you renew more than ever, and very often, the holy presumption of desiring from the Lord the grace to reach the holiness you would have attained had you always been faithful to his graces.*

Holy presumption—a blessed grace in the spiritual life, absolutely the opposite of discouragement in the spiritual life. It is never too late. The door to holiness is never closed. Do you feel with regret that you must settle for less? That you have not used well the years of your life thus far?

Then reread these words. Take to heart this counsel.

Ask that God turn your regret into holy presumption. Ask for this more than ever before. Ask for it not only often, but very often.

Ask for "the grace to reach the holiness you would have attained had you always been faithful to his graces."

> 20. *I am happy to hear of your resolution to see the will of God in everything, even in displeasing things. Do not be surprised if you see that you are not always constant in this resolution, because this is the nature of human acts, and this happens to all, since only in heaven will we be constant in our acts. You need only renew these peacefully and diligently when you feel yourself grow cold, just as you wash your face or hands again as needed, and do not expect that they always remain clean. Have the patience to do the same in the things of the soul, because this is the disposition of divine Providence, also for our greater good, because with the repetition of your acts, your merit multiplies.*

You resolve to try to see God's will in all that happens, even in difficult things, or to live the day in union with God, to respond to his call throughout the day. But it does not happen. Sometimes you do this; sometimes you do not; you are not constant in this practice.

Fulfillment of our spiritual resolutions, as is true of all human resolutions—to exercise regularly, to maintain a healthy diet, to practice faithfully a skill we seek to acquire—is not linear, and we must not be surprised that this is so. This is "the nature of human acts, and this happens to all." If you can deeply assimilate this truth, you will close the door to much discouragement.

How then to respond when you see your own inconstancy? "You need only renew these acts peacefully and diligently when you feel yourself grow cold." Peacefully. Diligently. Renew your resolution each time you feel it wane, and do so with peace. This is all you need to do.

As you work, do your hands or face grow dirty? You are not surprised, and you do not lose peace. You simply wash them and go on with the day. "Have the patience to do the same in the things of the soul." God's Providence is at work in this cycle of resolution, constancy mixed with inconstancy, and peaceful, patient renewal. Each time you do renew your resolution, he infuses all the more grace in your soul.

> 21. *Remember that we do not acquire holiness in twenty-four hours nor without continual defects and failings. The awareness that we will commit many failings, very many, greatly helps us toward holiness because it roots us in self-knowledge and in humility, and this is one of the foundations of our sanctification, the other being an invincible hope in divine mercy. Be attentive, then, not to allow yourself to be discouraged by any defect, and be always ready to begin at every moment. Only be faithful to this, and I promise you that you will become holy.*

"Seventy is the sum of our years, or eighty, if we are strong" (Ps. 90:10), and we need all of them, all the years God gives us, to become holy. "Remember that we do not acquire holiness in twenty-four hours." Do not put this burden on yourself, and do not let the enemy put it on you. He will try to discourage you, saying: "Look at you. Look at the years of your spiritual life and how far from holiness you are. What is wrong with you? Who are you to think that you will ever become holy?" "Remember that we do not acquire holiness in twenty-four hours." As St. John of the Cross says, "On this road we must always keep walking if we are to arrive" (*Ascent of Mount Carmel*, I, 11, 6).

Two things will help us to keep walking: humble self-knowledge and "an invincible hope in divine mercy." Invincible. This hope in God's ever-present and ever-loving mercy warms, encourages, and infuses energy for the journey.

"Be attentive, then, not to allow yourself to be discouraged by any defect, and be always ready to begin."

> *22. Remember that a single act of love of God wipes away our daily failings more easily and more quickly than tow catches fire.*

Tow is a fiber that catches fire easily and burns quickly. Imagine a match set to such a fabric — or perhaps to newspaper or other kindling. Watch it catch fire immediately and burn completely in only a moment. In an instant, it is no more.

"Remember that a single act of love of God wipes away our daily failings more easily and more quickly than tow catches fire." Today you did your best to be patient with your fellow workers, your children, your family, those with whom you live in community. You did your best to be attentive, to listen, to understand, to help. And that is enough to wipe away many faults.

> *23. Be aware that after a fall the evil spirit makes it seem difficult to return to ask God for forgiveness and almost impossible to correct the fault; on the contrary, the good spirit reduces the difficulty, makes it easy to obtain forgiveness, gives us energy, and encourages us, persuading us at the same time that we cannot be without faults, but that by means of these we must humble ourselves the more, and seek forgiveness from God.*

St. Ignatius writes that the enemy places obstacles, and the good spirit eases and takes away all obstacles (*Rules for the Discernment of Spirits*, Rule 2). When you have fallen into a defect or sin, you may feel a heavy sense that this will never change. You may hear insinuations like these: "You will just keep falling in this way. Here you are, yet again, with the same failing. You will always be the same. You will never change." This is the voice of the enemy! Recognize it as such, and reject it. *Never* believe this voice. It is the voice of the liar (John 8:44).

But when you have fallen, you will also hear another voice in your heart that says, "Do not hesitate to turn, now, to God. All you will find there is love, understanding, mercy, healing. It is easy to ask forgiveness of one who so loves you. He delights in pouring out upon you his healing love. And you can make progress in this failing. It is not so hard: God's grace will always be with you to strengthen you. Yes, you will struggle and will fall at times. This is the human condition. But these very falls can lead you to a blessed humility and to seek a forgiveness that makes you all the stronger." This is the voice of the good spirit! Recognize it as such, and accept it. Believe it, and be guided by it.

24. *Call to mind from time to time these words of Sacred Scripture: Behold the Lamb of God (John 1:29); I have not come to call the righteous, but sinners (Matt. 9:13); It is not those who are well that have need of the physician, but those who are ill (Matt. 9:12); If anyone has sinned we have an advocate with the Father (1 John 2:1); The Lord waits to show us his mercy and in forgiving you, he will be exalted (Isa. 30:18); All have sinned and have the need of the glory of God (Rom. 3:23); There will be greater joy in heaven for a sinner who repents than for ninety-nine just who have no need of repentance (Luke 15:7).*

   Continue to reflect on the parable of the Prodigal Son, on the Good Shepherd, on the way Jesus dealt with sinners, and finally on the outpouring of love with which he immolated himself on the cross and does yet every day on the altar. Let the conclusion be that we place ourselves immediately in God's presence, recognizing him as Father, hoping in him, never for a moment doubting that we shall be well received by so good a heavenly Father, and that he will generously forgive us, and that, indeed, we will be filled with his blessings.

OVERCOMING SPIRITUAL DISCOURAGEMENT

Take time right now, if you can, to read slowly through the seven Scripture verses cited. If it helps, take your Bible in hand, find each verse, and pray with it. Let each verse join with the others until an awareness of God's love and forgiveness wells up in your heart. Do this not once, but from time to time.

Then, right now if you can, later if you cannot, take your Bible, and turn to Luke 15. Read, ponder, and pray with the parable of the Prodigal Son: The Father runs, embraces, celebrates. Do the same with John 10, the parable of the Good Shepherd: I know my own; I lay down my life for them; no one can snatch them out of my hand. Then look at Jesus on the Cross, and see there his infinite love for you: "Having loved his own who were in the world, he loved them to the end" (John 13:1, RSVCE), to the last moment of his life, to the utmost self-giving. Look at a crucifix, perhaps take it in hand, and gaze upon it without hurry.

"Let the conclusion be that we place ourselves immediately in God's presence, recognizing him as Father, hoping in him, never for a moment doubting that we shall be well received by so good a heavenly Father; that he will generously forgive us; that, indeed, we will be filled with his blessings." Again Bruno's "immediately," and again his affirmation of the love in our Father's heart when we turn to him and ask forgiveness.

> 25. *I sense in your letter, which I was so happy to receive, a certain discouragement in the service of God. By the grace of God, beware of this. There is no enemy more to be feared than this.*

"There is no enemy to be feared more than this." Strong, clear, energizing words. Venerable Bruno repeats once more that discouragement—what St. Ignatius calls spiritual desolation—is the chief obstacle in the spiritual life. I believe that for most dedicated people, for most of the way on the spiritual journey, this is the real obstacle: times of discouragement and desolation when it is hard to go forward in prayer and God's service, when we find ourselves thinking unhappily of neglecting this or that in the spiritual life. There is no shame in experiencing such spiritual desolation. I repeat this because it is so important: There is *no shame* in experiencing such spiritual desolation! Every saint has. We all do. This is part of what it means to live in a fallen, yes, but loved and redeemed world. What matters is that we never give in to defeat.

"By the grace of God, beware of this!" Do you feel discouraged today? Do you find yourself spiritually desolate and disheartened? Do not simply allow this to continue!

How can we overcome such discouragement? We turn now to the concrete steps that Venerable Bruno proposes to this end.

Chapter Two

LIVING THE SPIRITUAL LIFE

26. *It is important to begin immediately to arrange with the priest for receiving Communion, and to do so as often as you can.*

Pope Benedict XVI writes, "A first essential setting for learning hope is prayer. When no one listens to me anymore, God still listens to me. When I can no longer talk to anyone or call upon anyone, I can always talk to God. When there is no longer anyone to help me deal with a need or expectation that goes beyond the human capacity for hope, he can help me" (*On Christian Hope*, 32).

And so, in this letter of spiritual direction, Venerable Bruno begins with prayer. The recipient is a mother of four children with a household to manage and financial difficulties to face.

The first thing is the Eucharist. Try, he says, to get to Mass and receive Holy Communion as often as you can, not only on Sunday but also during the week when possible. The Eucharist is the "source and summit of the Christian life" (Vatican II, cited in *Catechism of the Catholic Church*, 1324). It—that is, He—is the source of all our Christian strength and the summit, the center, the highest point of our Christian life. "For in the blessed Eucharist is contained the whole spiritual good of the Church, namely Christ himself" (ibid.). And so, Venerable Bruno says, begin here. Live as close to the Eucharist as you can.

*27. Be consistently faithful to meditation and to spiritual reading,
if it be only a quarter of an hour of meditation and a single
page of spiritual reading.*

First the Eucharist, then meditation. Venerable Bruno knows
that his correspondent's days—like yours—are packed. So, he
asks her, can you find just fifteen minutes a day for meditation, for
reflection and prayer on Scripture, on the truths of our Faith, these
most important truths on which our lives are based? Can you find
a quarter of an hour each day for this?

For some of us, this may be a part of the Liturgy of the Hours,
for others *lectio divina*, for others Ignatian reflective meditation
or imaginative contemplation of Scripture, for others the Rosary.
Whatever form we choose, whatever form most helps us, can we
find fifteen minutes a day for meditative prayer? What will happen
in our lives if we do?

And spiritual reading. Again the practicality: "if it be only a
single page." Can we read one page a day from a spiritual book?
Today this might also include watching a program on Catholic
television or listening to Catholic radio, podcasts, or audiobooks as
we exercise or drive. Venerable Bruno counsels that we let no day
pass without absorbing spiritual nourishment in a way compatible
with our daily commitments.

Hope is born of prayer.

*28. The same, too, for the examination of conscience, which
you can do while you are working.*

Then the examination of conscience, again with the same note
of practicality: It is an exercise of prayer that "you can do while
you are working." Finances weigh on us, the household calls for
attention, children have needs.... But do not forget to review your
day with God. When no other time is available, do this while your
hands are busy, but your mind can be free.

Venerable Bruno's approach to the daily spiritual life is already clear: Focus on the essential spiritual practices—Mass, meditation, spiritual reading, the examen. Choose an amount of time that you know you can sustain. Then be faithful—"you must be consistently faithful," he tells his correspondent. An excellent recipe for a lasting and fruitful spiritual life.

29. *Do not forget to raise your heart frequently, but gently and with peace, to God.*

Now Bruno turns to the rest of the day, the time of activity, the time beyond our formal times of prayer, and tells us to stay close to God during these hours. It is not hard. It takes no time from your tasks. Just raise your heart often, gently, with peace to God. Just a word or two in your heart, offering your work, your joy, your pain to him. Then, like Jesus, as your day unfolds, you will say the happiest words the human heart can say: "I am not alone" (John 16:32).

30. *Make acts of mortification, especially interior ones; for you, this means the effort to live each moment with a gentle and joyful spirit.*

A busy family life, responsibilities, worries, plans to make, problems to resolve, financial anxieties, concerns of health—amid all of this, impatience, sharpness, and irritability can so easily enter. To this woman, Venerable Bruno suggests that her mortification be interior, of the heart, "the effort to live each moment with a gentle and joyful spirit." *The effort.* Yes, this will require effort, a kind of mortification, a dying to self. And it will lift your heart and make of you a wellspring of harmony in the family and the community.

31. *For the love of God, I beg of you to wage continual warfare against negative moods, and never fail to begin again.*

"For the love of God," with all the energy I can, I beg of you the following: "Wage continual warfare against negative moods." Continual. Never simply give in to discouragement or heaviness of heart. Do battle against this temptation when you feel it. This is a blessed combat, a source of grace for you and peace for those with whom you live.

Once more we hear the call, almost a refrain, "Never fail to begin again." Now, as you read these words, today, this hour—*begin again*. God's love always awaits you, and the door is always open. It is not hard; it can be done in an instant. It can be done now.

32. *In going to the altar I will imagine seeing Simeon who went in the Spirit to the Temple for the presentation and circumcision of Jesus, or I will imagine seeing some other fervent saint.*

On the threshold of priestly ordination, Venerable Bruno outlined the way he desired to celebrate Mass. For each part of the Mass, he chose a corresponding affection of the heart, a theologically solid and biblically rich way to live the Mass. He maintained this practice throughout his life, and his timeless program speaks to us today. It can bless and make fruitful our own prayer of the Mass.

Some time ago, I printed his program and placed it near the altar where I celebrate Mass. Whenever I look at one or another of his suggestions, they help me live the Mass from the heart. They can help you as well.

But first, what is in our hearts as we leave home for Mass, as we enter the church, choose our pew, and settle ourselves for the liturgy?

"I will imagine seeing Simeon who went in the Spirit to the Temple for the presentation and circumcision of Jesus." Think of Simeon, filled with the Spirit, going to the Temple to meet the Savior he had so long desired, his heart overflowing with energy, longing, anticipation, thirsting for the encounter that would seal the meaning of his life. You, when you leave home and enter the church, go to meet the same Savior.

"Or I will imagine seeing some other fervent saint" entering the church for Mass. St. Teresa of Calcutta; St. Gianna Beretta Molla; the parents of St. Thérèse, Sts. Louis and Zèlie Martin; St. John Paul II; St. Thomas More; St. Elizabeth Seton; St. Monica … and so many other saints. What would we see if we watched them enter church for Mass? What filled their hearts as they did so? Faith, desire, love, awareness of a blessed privilege.

When I was a deacon, I served three of St. John Paul II's Masses. Each time, I watched him pray, simply drinking in the sight of one who prayed and loved the Mass so deeply. The blessed image of how he celebrated the Mass has remained with me through the years.

Today, tomorrow, or another day soon, you will be present at Mass. What is in your heart as you enter the church? Can you ask for the grace of sentiments like those of Simeon and other fervent saints? Can you ask to grow in this day by day, week by week?

33. *When Mass begins, in the penitential rite I will have the sentiments and the heart of the tax collector.*

"God, be merciful to me, a sinner" (Luke 18:13, RSVCE). Venerable Bruno invites us to seek "the sentiments and the heart" of this man, who stands at a distance, eyes lowered, hand to his breast, and repeats these words. When you say the words, "I confess to almighty God," and, "Lord, have mercy," can you ask for the same humble recognition of your need for forgiveness, for the same recourse to God's mercy? This man "went home justified" (Luke 18:14).

34. *At the Gloria the sentiments of the angels …*

When the Savior is born, the angels thrill with joy and sing God's praises: "Glory to God in the highest" (Luke 2:14). When you pray the Gloria at Mass, ask for a heart moved to praise God, to express joyfully, gratefully, your awareness of his saving love.

35. . . . at the Collect that of an ambassador for the Church . . .

When the priest says, "Let us pray," and then pronounces a prayer for the needs of the people, ask for a heart joined to his prayer, a heart that beseeches grace for so many people, for growth in faith and holiness, for so many needs.

36. . . . at the Readings and the Gospel those of a disciple . . .

"When he sat down his disciples came to him. And he opened his mouth and taught them" (Matt. 5:1–2, RSVCE). "The people pressed upon him to hear the word of God" (Luke 5:1, RSVCE). "All the people hung upon his words" (Luke 19:48, RSVCE). "You have the words of eternal life" (John 6:68, RSVCE). "No man ever spoke like this man!" (John 7:46, RSVCE).

When the Readings and the Gospel are proclaimed, listen like these disciples. Ask for a heart that is open, receptive, free from distractions, and attentive—one that allows God's word to penetrate, nourish, and transform.

"When the Sacred Scriptures are read in the Church, God himself speaks to his people, and Christ, present in his word, proclaims the Gospel" (*General Instruction of the Roman Missal*, 29). Venerable Bruno invites you to live this truth at Mass: When the Scriptures are read, be aware that God is speaking to us, *to you*; that Jesus is speaking to us, *to you*. Ask for the heart of a disciple, to be good soil in which the Word can bear fruit (Matt. 13:8, 23).

37. . . . at the Creed those of the martyrs . . .

Ask for the grace to say the Creed, the Profession of Faith—"I believe in one God . . . in one Lord Jesus Christ"—with the heart of a martyr, ready to give your life if necessary for this faith, this truth.

St. Justin Martyr and his companions stood before the Roman prefect Rusticus, who ordered them to offer sacrifice to the gods. In the name of all, Justin proclaimed their faith in Christ and refused to do as the official commanded: "The prefect Rusticus said: 'If you do not do as you are commanded you will be tortured without mercy.' Justin said: 'We hope to suffer torment for the sake of our Lord Jesus Christ, and so be saved'" (*Liturgy of the Hours*, 3, 1448–1449). Their martyrdom followed.

Ask for the grace to proclaim the Creed with the heart of a martyr.

38. . . . at the Offertory those of Melchizedek . . .

Melchizedek offered bread and wine (Gen. 14:18) and is seen as an Old Testament foreshadowing of Christ (Heb. 7), who offers himself in the form of bread and wine. The Letter to the Hebrews says of Christ, "You are a priest forever according to the order of Melchizedek" (Heb. 7:17).

You, too, are a priest. In your baptism, you were given a share in the priesthood of the faithful:

> The baptized, by regeneration and the anointing of the Holy Spirit, are consecrated as a spiritual house and a holy priesthood, in order that through all those works which are those of the Christian they may offer spiritual sacrifices and proclaim the power of him who has called them out of darkness into his marvelous light. Therefore all the disciples of Christ, persevering in prayer and praising God, should present themselves as a living sacrifice, holy and pleasing to God. (Vatican II, *Constitution on the Church*, 10)

At the offertory, when the gifts and the altar are prepared, ask for a heart that offers to God, in union with Christ's self-offering, the "living sacrifice, holy and pleasing to God" of your whole life with its joys and sorrows, its responsibilities and tasks—all that you are and all that you do.

39. . . . at the Preface those of the blessed in heaven . . .

After this I had a vision of a great multitude, which no one could count, from every nation, race, people, and tongue. They stood before the throne and before the Lamb, wearing white robes and holding palm branches in their hands. They cried out in a loud voice: 'Salvation comes from our God, who is seated on the throne, and from the Lamb.' All the angels stood around the throne and around the elders and the four living creatures. They prostrated themselves before the throne, worshiped God, and exclaimed: 'Amen. Blessing and glory, wisdom and thanksgiving, honor, power, and might be to our God forever and ever. Amen.' (Rev. 7:9–12).

In the Preface of the Mass, we pray, "And so, with Angels and Archangels, with Thrones and Dominions, and with all the Hosts and Powers of heaven, we sing the hymn of your glory, as without end we acclaim, 'Holy, holy, holy....'"

When you pray these words, ask for a heart like that of the Blessed in heaven, a heart filled with adoration and praise to the God who so loves you and who is present to you.

40. . . . at the Consecration those of Christ . . .

In this sublime moment of the Mass, seek a heart like that of Christ in his self-offering: "This is my body ... This is my blood of the covenant, which will be shed on behalf of many for the forgiveness of sins" (Matt. 26:26–28).

Seek a heart like that of Christ in his self-giving for his people: "I am the good shepherd. A good shepherd lays down his life for the sheep" (John 10:11). "He loved his own in the world and he loved them to the end" (John 13:1). "He emptied himself, taking the form of a slave" (Phil. 2:7). "Father, if it is possible, let this cup pass from me; yet, not as I will, but as you will" (Matt. 26:39).

Let your heart be stilled. Let it reach the deep point. Let it be aware of the self-offering of Jesus. Let it unite with Jesus, offering with him your own self, your own life, to the Father.

> *41. ... at the Our Father those of one who asks for what he needs ...*

Here is one who is in need and who asks for help, who has no other recourse than simply to beg, who holds out his hand, who silently waits upon the goodness of the one before him.

As you pray the Our Father, ask for a heart that seeks, entreats, begs for what it needs, knowing the love of the Father to whom it addresses this prayer: "Our Father ... Give us this day ... forgive us ... lead us not ... deliver us."

> *42. ... at the Lamb of God those of one who is guilty and in need of forgiveness ...*

The words Venerable Bruno uses signify one who is guilty of wrongdoing, is accused of it, and is brought to judgement. Again and again, this person raises a heartfelt plea for mercy and forgiveness.

At this point in the Mass, we do the same: "Lamb of God ... have mercy," "Lamb of God ... have mercy," "Lamb of God ... grant us peace." Seek a humble heart, a heart that pleads for the infinite mercy of the Lamb of God whose one desire is to pour out that mercy upon you.

This is the Lamb of God who takes away the sins of the world, who takes away *our* sins.

> *43. ... at Communion those of one in love ...*

Servant of God Elisabeth Leseur describes her reception of Communion on one occasion:

> I went to Communion in the chapel of the Blessed Sacrament. Those moments were completely and supernaturally happy. I felt in myself the living presence of the blessed Christ, of God himself, bringing me an ineffable love; this incomparable Soul spoke to mine, and all the infinite tenderness of the Savior passed for an instant into me. Never will this divine trace be effaced. The triumphant Christ, the eternal Word, He who as man has suffered and loved, the one living God, took possession of my soul for all eternity in that unforgettable moment. I felt myself renewed to my very depths by him, ready for a new life, for duty, for the work intended by his Providence. I gave myself without reserve, and I gave him the future. (My *Spirit Rejoices*, 73–74)

"At Communion those of one in love." When you receive Communion, as you approach the altar, as you receive, when you return to your place, when you make your thanksgiving—ask for the heart of one in love.

Now all commentary must be silent and withdraw. You are alone with the One who loves you.

44. . . . at the "Go forth, the Mass is ended" those of an apostle.

"Those assembled are sent forth to bring the fruits of the Eucharist to the world" (*General Instruction of the Roman Missal*, Concluding Rites).

You are an apostle—the word means "one who is sent"—sent forth to your family, your workplace, the people in your life, the world, to bring the grace, the blessing, the light, the fruits of the Mass just concluded. As you rise, walk down the aisle, head to your car, and drive home, do so with this awareness in your heart, with this readiness. Bring the grace of the Mass with you, and bring it to a world that so desperately needs it.

"Go, therefore, and make disciples of all nations" (Matt. 28:19).

45. I will go forth from the altar as if breathing fire.

This is Venerable Bruno's desire, his prayer. It can be yours. When you can, return to his proposal for each part of the Mass. Look at one or another from time to time. With simplicity, try to live these. Seek the grace of quiet growth in these sentiments over the days, weeks, and years. If you do, Mass will become ever more the "source and summit" of your spiritual life. And your hope, your consolation, will grow.

> *46. I rejoice, and I thank the Lord from my heart that you were able to make your spiritual retreat without exterior distractions and in peace, as this is a great grace from the good God. I approve very strongly your three resolutions: 1. purity of intention will unite you all the more to God and will also spare you many sorrows that ordinarily come from seeking oneself and not God; a holy tenacity, in the second place, in never omitting even a little of your daily prayer and your other spiritual practices will discourage the enemy from increasing the difficulty of doing them, with the purpose of leading you to omit some of them; 3. the decision always to begin will close the door to discouragement, and that of itself will free you from tepidity and from past faults.*

Seek to please God, to give God joy, in your daily actions. This "purity of intention" will bring you close to God throughout the day and spare you many sorrows.

"A holy tenacity." Once more, Venerable Bruno encourages you to choose nourishing practices of prayer, to choose a sustainable amount of time for them, and then to be *tenacious*—with a holy tenacity—in maintaining them. We "ought always to pray and not lose heart" (Luke 18:1, RSVCE).

"The decision always to begin again" will be your remedy against any discouragement. Are you discouraged today? Now? Begin again! Now! This "will close the door to discouragement."

> 47. I thank you from my heart for the good wishes for this year expressed to the Lord on my behalf. I have not failed to do the same for you at the altar. For the rest, do not let yourself be discouraged even a little. Be sure that your proposals regarding your spiritual practices will not be without effect and will gain for you many graces in this year. Bear the burden only of seeing the defects of your soul, but rather than be disappointed, seek always to encourage your soul to begin, but gently, as St. Francis de Sales prescribed for you, who loved to see us practice gentleness not only toward others but also toward ourselves.

Again and again, do not let yourself be discouraged "even a little." Do not accept even that little troubling, nagging hesitation that does not stop your service of God, but does hamper it, does weigh on it. And be sure that your efforts to grow spiritually "will not be without effect and will gain you many graces."

Yes, when you see your defects—your impatience, your failures to listen and to help, the limits of your prayer—you will feel the burden of them, but do not be disappointed or discouraged. Rather, "seek always to encourage your soul to begin," but gently, with gentleness not only toward others but also toward yourself.

Are you gentle toward yourself? If you are gentle toward others when they fail and are discouraged, if you are a presence that encourages them at such times, can you be this also toward yourself? "Learn from me; for I am gentle and lowly in heart" (Matt. 11:29, RSVCE).

St. Francis de Sales writes, "Believe me, my daughter, as a parent's tender, affectionate remonstrance has far more weight with his child than anger and sternness, so when we judge our own heart guilty, if we treat it gently, rather in a spirit of pity than anger, encouraging it to amendment, its repentance will be much deeper and more lasting than if stirred up in vehemence and wrath" (*Introduction to the Devout Life*, III, 9).

> 48. *I will go to Confession and receive Communion every eight days as I have done for many years. These sacraments are the channels that God has established to communicate to me his graces and his light. Therefore my perseverance depends upon the faithful practice of them. When I approach these sacraments, I will ask insistently of my Lord the help I need to fulfill the obligations of my state of life.*

These words are found in a spiritual program for a married woman. Confession and Communion: "These sacraments are the channels that God has established to communicate to me his graces and his light." In Venerable Bruno's time, when Communion was often received once a year, his counsel was bold: Go to Mass and receive Communion as often as you can.

Add regular Confession according to the rhythm that is right for you. Over the years, I have seen the difference between infrequent and regular Confession. In the first case, grace is received, but the infrequency does not allow one Confession to build on another. In the second, grace builds upon grace, and continuing progress results.

Five benefits derive from this practice: "The regular confession of our venial sins helps us form our conscience, fight against evil tendencies, let ourselves be healed by Christ, and progress in the life of the Spirit. By receiving more frequently through this sacrament the gift of the Father's mercy, we are spurred to be merciful as he is merciful" (*Catechism of the Catholic Church*, 1458). Spiritual formation. Aid in battling evil tendencies. Healing by Christ. Progress in the Spirit. Growth in mercy toward others. Who would not want these?

Is regular Confession a part of your life? Could it be?

Confession and Communion. These two sacraments are the channels of God's grace and light to us. If you stay close to them, you will find the help you need to fulfill the responsibilities of your state of life—marriage, parenting, work in the world, the single condition, priesthood, religious life. Do you not need this help?

> 49. *I will be faithful in making fifteen minutes of meditation every day and fifteen minutes of spiritual reading and the examination of conscience in the evening. I will also attend Mass if I can. It is very right that I give an hour of the day to God when the obligations of my state of life permit it.*

Further words of spiritual counsel to a married woman. Can you, in your vocation, do this? Will the "obligations of your state of life"—your duties, your responsibilities in the family, at work, in service to others—permit it? Fifteen minutes of meditation a day. Fifteen minutes of spiritual reading. The examen prayer in the evening. Daily Mass when possible. Do your duties permit you to give one hour a day to prayer in this way? "A first essential setting for learning hope is prayer" (Benedict XVI).

> 50. *Because of this I can never recommend enough to you the daily meditation of the holy truths of our religion, made with real commitment, with the heart, and continued with a holy tenacity, and always, as much as possible, at a fixed hour of the day. It will be easier to maintain this practice if you also do spiritual reading daily with calm reflection and on well-chosen spiritual books.*

This counsel was given to a married layman. Again, daily meditation, "made with real commitment, with the heart, and continued with a holy tenacity."

Venerable Bruno offers practical advice that will make this commitment easier: "always, as much as possible, at a fixed hour of the day." Upon rising? Before or after Mass? On your lunch hour? After work? Just before retiring? During the commute on the train or subway? Find a time that works for you, and try to be faithful to it.

Another help to do this: "It will be easier to maintain this practice if you also do spiritual reading daily with calm reflection and on well-chosen spiritual books."

> 51. *I propose never to omit my meditation and always to do it with method and fidelity.*

These are words from the personal spiritual notes of the young Bruno. Meditation without fail. And done with two things: method and fidelity. Again the same counsel: Make solid and sustainable choices about your program of prayer (method), and then be faithful (fidelity).

> 52. *Method for spiritual reading: after the choice of a book and after having chosen the time for this reading, begin the reading by raising my heart to God, confident that God himself speaks to us through the book; that it is a letter he sends to us from his heavenly dwelling. Ask of him an attentive and docile heart, and the grace to understand these truths well so as to profit spiritually by them. Then read with attention and without hurry, pausing on those truths that speak more to our present needs and returning from time to time to our own heart and to the God who is speaking to us. Never finish the reading without some holy resolution.*

For your spiritual reading or listening (book, podcast, video), choose the material and the time for it.

Now attentively reread Venerable Bruno's words about how to do this reading (or listening or viewing). How might you begin? How might you read or listen or view? How might you finish? A heart raised to God, with confidence, attention, docility, without hurry, with pauses, returning from time to time to the heart, remembering to identify a fruit to take from each reading. Can you do this? Grow in this day by day? What will happen if you do?

53. *Every day a chapter of the Gospel of Jesus Christ for reading, and buy a small edition of the New Testament for myself. A great means, easy and powerful for resisting temptation, is to use the Word of God, which is so holy, efficacious, and powerful, as we see in the example of Jesus Christ.*

Another personal practice of the young Bruno that could bless us today. Read a chapter every day from the Gospels, and have a small copy (print or digital) of the Gospels always with you. This is, Venerable Bruno tells us, "a great means, easy and powerful for resisting temptation" and for growth in love of Jesus. This Word is "holy," "efficacious," and "powerful"—the Word that Jesus used to overcome temptation (Matt. 4:1–11).

"The force and power in the word of God is so great that it stands as the support and energy of the Church, the strength of faith for her sons, the food of the soul, the pure and everlasting source of spiritual life" (Vatican II, *Constitution on Divine Revelation*, 21). "The strength of faith for her sons," "food for the soul," a "pure and everlasting source of spiritual life"—three spiritual riches we all need.

The Church, therefore, "earnestly and especially urges all the Christian faithful ... to learn by frequent reading of the divine Scriptures the 'excellent knowledge of Jesus Christ' (see Phil. 3:8)" (Vatican II, *Constitution on Divine Revelation*, 25).

54. *I will read St. Theresa, pursuing this reading until I have
read all of her works. I will also always carry with me the*
Imitation of Christ *or the* Spiritual Combat *in order to
read them in free moments or when I feel need of it, and I
will read a chapter from them randomly. I will do this reading
in an unhurried and attentive way.*

A further spiritual proposal of the young Bruno. Years ago, real-
izing that I could not read all the spiritual writing available, I made
the decision to focus on the classics: St. Augustine, St. Teresa of
Avila, St. John of the Cross, St. Thérèse, St. Francis de Sales, St.
Bonaventure, St. Catherine of Siena, St. John Henry Newman,
Brother Lawrence of the Resurrection, and others. It was one of the
best decisions I have ever made, and I feel the fruits of it continually.

Here, the young Bruno makes that decision—decades earlier
in life than I did! As I have read his writings over the years, I have
seen how familiar he grew with the richest texts of our spiritual
tradition.

He focused on *The Imitation of Christ,* "the best loved book by
Christians after the Bible" (Father Rainero Cantalamessa, O.F.M.
Cap.), and Lorenzo Scupoli's *Spiritual Combat,* another esteemed
classic of our tradition. Bruno wished always to have solid spiritual
nourishment with him, available in need or simply to enrich free
moments.

Have you read any of the saints' writings? Do you have spiritual
nourishment at hand when you need it? In times of struggle, of
temptation? When you desire simply to be with and deepen your
relationship with God? Lists of such writings abound, and a simple
web search will bring up many of them. Find those books that most
feed you spiritually, and read them.

55. *The Spiritual Exercises of St. Ignatius are in general, a most
powerful instrument of divine grace for the universal reform*

*of the world, and in particular, a sure method by which
everyone can become a saint, a great saint, and quickly.*

Do you ever make a retreat? Would it be possible to get away
for a weekend once a year? For even a day or a part of a day? Does
your parish host such times of prayer? Is there a retreat house within
traveling distance? Retreats can be powerful occasions of encouragement and renewal.

Venerable Bruno especially loved the Spiritual Exercises of
St. Ignatius; he considered the Ignatian retreat "a most powerful
instrument of divine grace" for the renewal of the world, "a sure
method by which everyone can become a saint, a great saint, and
quickly." We need only persevere after the retreat. The Spiritual
Exercises can be adapted to all situations in life: a weekend, a few
days, or several more in a retreat house; an hour of prayer daily at
home over several months; a parish mission.

Have you ever considered an Ignatian retreat? I remember that
when I finished my own Ignatian retreat, I said to myself, "Someone
has finally taught me how to pray." The blessing of that retreat, now
forty years past, remains with me constantly. Giving such retreats, I
have witnessed the truth of what Venerable Bruno affirms, that they
are indeed "a most powerful instrument of divine grace" and help
all who make them to "become a saint, a great saint, and quickly."

56. *At times I find myself in spirit in your Villa at Fiesole, deeply
regretting that we cannot be together there again this year as
last, because nothing in this world is of such great value as
the opportunity to spend several days in peace occupied only
with the great matters in life: God, the soul, and eternity.*

The preceding year, Venerable Bruno had traveled to Florence
and given the Spiritual Exercises there. Now he writes to one
who participated in that retreat, desirous of doing so again in the

current year, "because nothing in this world is of such great value as the opportunity to spend several days in peace occupied only with the great matters in life: God, the soul, and eternity." God. The soul. Eternity.

Do you ever have that opportunity? Might it be possible?

Chapter Three

LIVING THE DAY WITH JESUS

57. God has placed me in this state of life; in this and no other
I must serve him and be saved. All the circumstances and
events in my state of life, such as the different characters
of the persons with whom I interact, the events that take
place, the times and places in which these occur, reveal the
order of Providence through which the Lord has willed to
work my salvation. I must adapt myself to all these things
and not think that I can force them to adapt themselves to
me. And so, I will try always to adapt to these with peace
and joy of heart, confident that God knows better than I
what is best for me.

Venerable Bruno writes to a married woman and voices convic-
tions of faith to guide her — and all of us — in our respective states
of life: "God has placed me in this state of life; in this and no other
I must serve him and be saved." The people in your life — these,
and not others; the places in your life — these, and not others; the
daily tasks appointed to you — these, and not others: Your circumstances of life "reveal the order of Providence through which the
Lord has willed to work your salvation."

Does your heart desire holiness? Closeness with God? Eternal
life? You already have all that you need to progress toward these.

"If only I were ... If only I had ... If only it were not for ..." No. You already have all that you need to love and serve God.

"I must adapt myself to all these things and not think that I can force them to adapt themselves to me." Open your heart to your husband, to your wife, to your children, to your daily tasks, to your work, to your life in the parish, to your community. Love these people, in these circumstances. "God has placed me in this state of life; in this and no other I must serve him and be saved."

St. Edith Stein says, "Whatever did not fit in with my plan did lie within the plan of God. I have an ever deeper and firmer belief that nothing is an accident when seen in the light of God, that my whole life down to the smallest details has been marked out for me in the plan of Divine Providence and has a completely coherent meaning in God's all-seeing eyes" (*The Journey: A Guide for the Modern Pilgrim*, 26).

> 58. *Let him walk at the pace that God wishes in all his spiritual practices, however holy they may be, and neither hurry ahead nor hold back from this rate of progress.*

These words of the young Bruno have stayed in my mind through the years. I like them because they keep me — at least when I am spiritually attentive! — from placing on myself a pressure that God does not want me to carry. We should neither "hurry ahead," trying to do more and go faster than God wants, with all the strain this involves, nor "hold back," delaying, vacillating, when we sense God calling us to the next step: "Let him walk at the pace that God wishes in all his spiritual practices."

A serene confidence thus enters our spiritual lives.

> 59. *I would like to take the opportunity of the departure from Turin of your son for some profit, but I do not know what I should say: Should I praise you for your fidelity to God?*

Ought I chide you? I do not know at all. So I will take a sure part and that is to urge you to begin each day, leaving the past to the mercy of the Lord and the future to his Divine Providence. In the meantime, consider every day that the good God has entrusted you with a mission. In regard to temporal matters, never let anything trouble you, and the same with respect to your faults, taking care to counter them immediately by an act of love of God. Be attentive to practice the virtues of patience and gentleness; you can make a special examination on this in the evening and at midday.

A young man, studying in the city, is returning home to visit his family. His mother is under the spiritual direction of Venerable Bruno, who takes the opportunity to send her a note of spiritual encouragement.

Not knowing how things stand with her, Venerable Bruno decides to "take a sure part." As we might expect, he invites her — and us — "to begin each day, leaving the past to the mercy of the Lord and the future to his Divine Providence." Can you really leave the past to God's mercy? All of your past? St. John Vianney says, "Our faults are grains of sand beside the mountain of the mercy of God." And can you leave the future, with all its uncertainties and worries, to the Divine Providence of God? St. John Henry Newman says, "I do not ask to see/ The distant scene — one step enough for me."

Sometimes, when I find myself worried about the future, I look back over my life. Again and again, I see the pattern: how I worried about things and how, in retrospect, I see that God carried me safely through them all. When I do this, my heart lifts. I find more peace and new hope that God will see me through the challenge that lies ahead. "Leave the past to the mercy of the Lord and the future to his Divine Providence."

Today, then. What lies ahead in the hours of this day, the day that you are reading this? "Consider every day that the good God has entrusted you with a mission." What mission has God entrusted to you today? To complete these tasks? To care for these family members? To help this person? To do the shopping and to prepare a meal?

I find my heart lifting as I write these words. Venerable Bruno's counsel makes things so simple and clear. Leave the past to God's mercy, the future to his Providence. You have today. You have a mission this day from God. Seek, with peace, to fulfill it. That is all God asks. That is all you need to do.

> 60. *Way of carrying out the actions of every day: Regarding the manner of carrying out our daily actions, we follow the only one pleasing to God and proposed to us by the Eternal Father, that is, the imitation of God's own Son who made himself a servant so as to be the model of his servants. In every action, then, we keep Jesus Christ before our eyes, taking him as our companion and model, and seeking to imitate him in the most perfect way, both outwardly and inwardly, together with the example of the Most Blessed Virgin. In this way, with the intercession of Mary, we become ever more like the image of Jesus, which we must impress upon our souls.*

You began the day with prayer. Now you are immersed in the thousand activities of the day. One task follows another. Emails require responses. Phone calls must be made. You need to drive for an errand. Household tasks, projects at work, family concerns, financial issues, doctors' appointments—the day unfolds in the midst of these many activities and preoccupations. How do you live them? How do you handle them? Is there a way to live them in union with Jesus? To remain united with Jesus in the midst of this activity? Venerable Bruno addresses this question with his habitual practicality. In this quotation and the next, he traces a faith-filled "way of carrying out the actions of every day."

When I was a seminarian, our novice master cited these words of Venerable Bruno as one of his greatest gifts to us, words that reveal the heart of his sanctity. I quoted them at the conclusion of *Begin Again*, the biography I wrote of Venerable Bruno. They moved me as I quoted them and often do still. Our novice master was right; these words do manifest Venerable Bruno's heart, and they are a gift to all who live full and pressured days.

As always with Bruno, the approach is simple, practical, and rich: Just stay close to Jesus in each action. "In every action we keep Jesus Christ before our eyes, taking him as our companion and model, and seeking to imitate him in the most perfect way." Does that seem lovely but too generic to be of help? Venerable Bruno immediately provides, in the next few selections, a simple, concrete way of doing this, of living each action with Jesus. This way involves how we begin each action, how we carry it out, and how we conclude it. If, further, we look to the example of and seek the intercession of Mary, we will be strengthened in this effort.

> 61. *And the better to succeed in this undertaking, we undertake always to begin the action not impetuously, but with faith, that is, with a peaceful look of faith toward Jesus, our model. We clothe ourselves in his spirit and unite ourselves to his will, in order to act as he would have done in similar circumstances.*

You are about to leave home for work. You are beginning a time of study. You are setting out to go shopping. You are heading to church for an activity. You are beginning to prepare supper. Or starting any significant activity of the day. How do you begin this activity? "Not impetuously, but with faith"—that is, not unreflectively, simply carried along by the flow of the day, but with faith. More specifically, Venerable Bruno says, "with a peaceful look of faith toward Jesus, our model."

As you walk out the door toward the car, as you sit down to begin your study, as you walk across the parking lot to the church, as you put on the apron … simply lift your spiritual gaze to Jesus, clothing yourself in his spirit and uniting yourself to his will. This adds no time to the activity, but it changes everything.

62. *We carry out the action not indifferently, but with affection, with frequent peaceful and serenely confident glances of the heart towards Jesus.*

You are working on the project as the morning unfolds, you are in the midst of preparing supper, you are doing the shopping … and, from time to time, you lift your heart to Jesus with peace and trust. Again, everything changes. You are not alone. You are with Jesus.

I remember reading the life of St. Marie of the Incarnation. When she was a girl, one day she watched her mother as she went about her daily tasks and saw that her lips were moving silently as she worked, praying, in communion with God. "We carry out the action … with affection, with frequent peaceful and serenely confident glances of the heart towards Jesus." As I write this, I hear afresh the call to live this way.

63. *We finish the action not abruptly but with reflection, that is, with a brief look to see if the action was wholly according to the Heart of Jesus or not, so as to thank Our Lord or express our contrition. We set ourselves to do this always, whether it be a question of praying, acting, or enduring and suffering.*

The morning's project is complete. You have returned from the errands. Supper is now ready. You conclude the action "not abruptly but with reflection, that is, with a brief look to see if the action was wholly according to the Heart of Jesus." Again, this adds no time to the action, but it changes so much. With Jesus, you look briefly over the task. Was it done according to his Heart? With love? With care? With patience? With attention to others? If so, thank Jesus; if not, ask forgiveness.

What will happen if, with all our limitations, with all our remembering and forgetting, we sincerely try to begin, carry out, and finish the main actions of the day in this way?

64. *The fruits that arise from this way of acting—this grace that we unceasingly ask of Jesus and Mary—consist in a great likeness to Jesus and union with him, in which lies our entire sanctification. To this end, we constantly seek to keep our memory from empty wandering and tranquilly fixed on Jesus, our mind accustomed to see and judge everything according to Jesus, and our will always peacefully united to Jesus. In short, in this way we always live in Jesus's company, we always speak with Jesus, we are always united with Jesus in our intentions and our actions, and so become living copies of Jesus.*

Living copies of Jesus. Always in Jesus's company. Always speaking with Jesus. Always united with Jesus in our intentions and our actions. "O God, you are my God—it is you I seek! For you my body yearns; for you my soul thirsts" (Ps. 63:2). "You have made us for yourself, O God, and our hearts are restless until they rest in you" (St. Augustine). "Only God satisfies" (St. Thomas Aquinas).

Here is a simple and easy way to live with Jesus in the actions of every day, always with Jesus, always speaking with him. Will you not try this?

65. *Thus Jesus becomes the sole treasure of our hearts. Jesus dwells in our hearts, and we live in the Heart of Jesus. Is there anything greater or more consoling than this?*

"Is there anything greater or more consoling than this?" Is there? And it can be yours. The way, as Venerable Bruno says here, is not difficult. It only requires beginning, carrying out, and finishing our principal daily actions in the way he describes.

I have always loved Jesus's words, "I am not alone" (John 16:32, RSVCE). As St. Paul VI comments, "If Jesus radiates such peace, such assurance, such happiness, such availability, it is by reason of the inexpressible love by which he knows that he is loved by his Father" (*On Christian Joy*, 1975, III). Not to be alone! To know that someone is there and understands!

One day, several years ago, I was scheduled for surgery. I awoke early that morning aware that something was wrong. The pain increased, and I called the emergency number that the surgeon had given me. The doctor who answered misunderstood the symptoms, and the remedies he suggested did not help. Finally, I asked one of the priests to call an ambulance. I will never forget the minutes of waiting in the worst pain I had ever felt. One of our priests stood by the bed, just stood there, waiting with me, being with me. His presence meant more than I can ever say. I was not alone.

Venerable Bruno tells us gently, warmly, insistently, and with practical wisdom that we are not alone, that we can live the actions of the day with Jesus, in his company, speaking with him, united with him. "Is there anything greater or more consoling than this?"

66. *We will seek always to recall these words of Sacred Scripture as our norm: "He will not cry out, nor shout, nor make his voice heard in the street" (Isa. 42:2); "Learn from me, for I am meek and humble of heart; and you will find rest for your souls" (Matt. 11:29); "Love one another with mutual affection; anticipate one another in showing honor" (Rom. 12:10).*

How do you interact with your spouse? Your children? Your parents? Your colleagues? Other parishioners? Community members? Fellow priests? Reread each of the three biblical passages Venerable Bruno cites here. Ponder them. Pray about them. Can you, as he asks, take them as your norm?

In a sermon, Gerard Manley Hopkins says, "From all that might be said of Christ's character, I single out one point and beg you to notice that. He loved to praise, he loved to reward. He knew what was in man, he best knew men's faults, and yet he was warmest in their praise."

"Learn from me."

67. *Peace of heart, a joyful spirit, love of neighbor, compassion for the sorrows of others, goodness of heart, patience, forbearance with others, a warm manner, acceptance of others' desires that are not of offense to God: that is, to be gentle and lowly of heart. This is the character I propose to have and that I will continually ask of the Sacred Heart of Jesus and of Mary.*

Words found in a program of spiritual life Venerable Bruno composed for a married woman. These words simply apply to family living Jesus's self-description as "gentle and lowly of heart" (Matt. 11:29, RSVCE). What would your marriage be like if you sought this character from Jesus, through Mary's intercession? Your family home? Your religious community? Your rectory and parish?

"Compassion for the sorrows of others, goodness of heart, patience, forbearance with others, a warm manner,… This is the character I propose to have." And all this in the many small, daily interactions of life. You can give such great encouragement and lift the spirits of others so much in this way.

68. *I am happy to learn that you experience many good and holy desires. Be sure that none will be left without its reward. If*

you give constant and loving attention to the inspirations of God throughout the day, he will multiply these inspirations, and you will be well recompensed for your times of dryness in your meditations.

"Constant and loving attention to the inspirations of God throughout the day." Jean Pierre de Caussade, in his *Abandonment to Divine Providence*, writes:

There is never a moment when God does not come forward in the guise of some suffering or some duty, and all that takes place within us, around us, and through us both includes and hides his activity. Yet, because it is invisible, we are always taken by surprise and do not recognize his operation until it has passed by us. If we could lift the veil, and if we watched with vigilant attention, God would endlessly reveal himself to us, and we should see and rejoice in his active presence in all that befalls us. At every event we should exclaim: 'It is the Lord!' (John 21:7, RSVCE). Nothing could happen to us without our accepting it as a gift from God.

Is it true that we are always taken by surprise and do not recognize God's operation until it has passed by us? What if the gap between God's inspirations in the moment and the time when we realize what he was offering diminished, almost disappeared, so that we could perceive in the moment itself—when, for example, this person approaches and asks for help, when events take an unforeseen turn, when plans do not turn out in the way hoped, and similar—what God is offering and where God is leading? "If we could lift the veil, and if we watched with vigilant attention, God would endlessly reveal himself to us, and we should see and rejoice in his active presence in all that befalls us."

Are you familiar with the examen prayer? Could you pray this prayer that fosters attention to God's action in the day? As you grow more aware of God constantly at work in your day, experience will show you why Venerable Bruno so warmly encourages "constant and loving attention to the inspirations of God throughout the day."

69. *I will plan the activities of my day so that I may more surely do the will of God and give him glory in all that I do: not different things, but the same things done differently; not doing things simply out of habit, but out of love.*

"Not different things, but the same things done differently." In daily life, most often this is our path to holiness: not to search for different occupations, but to do the things we always have in a different, more faith-inspired, more Christ-centered, more loving way. St. Zélie Martin, the mother of St. Thérèse of Lisieux, grew to heroic holiness through her marriage, her care of her children, and her lace-making business that supported the family. Zélie's letters center on these seemingly mundane matters, through which she became a saint. "Not different things, but the same things done differently."

"Not doing things simply out of habit, but out of love." Not out of habit, just because these tasks must be done, but out of love, choosing these tasks, doing them with the power of love that God has given us. The journey from habit to love is great. Ask for this grace, seek it, and let it bless your life and give you joy.

70. *I wish you every true good, and I am consoled in seeing you ever more dedicated to the glory of God, since, in this world, there is no purpose greater than this, and none more consoling.*

Venerable Bruno rejoices to see this layman dedicated, in his family life and active service, to the glory of God. What does Bruno understand by "the glory of God"? God is glorified when human hearts come to know and love him in this world, and so prepare an eternity of blessed communion with him. This layman's life serves to lead others to God, and Venerable Bruno rejoices to see it, "since, in this world, there is no purpose greater than this, and none more consoling."

Such is the deepest meaning of your life as well, and in it you will find your greatest consolation: that through faithfully living your vocation, through your prayer, through your service of others, through the joys and sorrows of your life, you help human hearts to know and love God and so to enter eternal life.

St. Ignatius of Loyola says, "God created us out of love so that we might praise and reverence his infinite goodness, and by dedicating our lives to his service, might enter an eternity of joyful communion with him" (*Principle and Foundation, a Contemporary Reading*).

> 71. *Oh, how great a thing it is, and how consoling, to serve as an instrument to glorify God!*

Venerable Bruno lays bare his own heart, a heart that thrills to consider the greatness of living in such a way that our lives give glory to God—that they lead others to God. "Oh, how great a thing it is, and how consoling!" That cry of his heart is an encouragement to the recipient of this letter, and to us.

> 72. *Allow me to continue to recommend to you that you take good care of your health, especially by giving at least a part of your tasks to others so as to have, in the course of the week, some moments of peace. Otherwise the bow that is always bent will finally break. And be sure that the Christian Friendship has great need of you, so that the greater glory of God also requires this same care for your health.*

In a similar vein, St. Teresa of Avila writes, "Take care, then, of the body for the love of God, because at many times the body must serve the soul" (*Life*, X, 23). When I first saw this sentence, it struck me, and I have remembered it ever since. Take care of the body, take care of the health God has given you. Why? Many answers may be given to that question, and many are given today. For St. Teresa, the answer is clear: "for the love of God." She explains, "because at many times the body must serve the soul."

To this dedicated layman, whose service was so important to his family and the work of the Christian Friendship association, Venerable Bruno likewise recommends care of his health, that he ensure at least some moments of peace, of genuine leisure, in the week. Much like St. Teresa, Venerable Bruno explains "that the greater glory of God also requires this same care for your health."

Do you see your health as a gift of God? As necessary for the calling God has given you in the years of your life? Do you take wise care of it for the love of God, for his greater glory?

Chapter Four

LIVING THE CROSS AND RESURRECTION OF JESUS

73. *With regard to your interior battles and the empty thoughts you find in yourself, be patient with yourself and remain in peace; give these little weight. Bear with them as if they were noisy persons quarrelling in the streets outside. And if you find the courage for this as well, humble yourself before God and thank him for these things that humble you and begin to make you more like him. Say to him, "It was good for me to be afflicted, that I might learn your statutes" [Ps. 119:71]. Seek all this in your heart; as regards your interactions with others, express your reasons peacefully and with gentleness, and do not let yourself be disturbed.*

Restless thoughts, empty thoughts, thoughts that burden you —and you so long to be free of them, feeling humiliated that you cannot seem to overcome them even with your best efforts. "Be patient with yourself and remain in peace; give these little weight."

Noisy people quarrelling in the street outside; their voices are unwelcome, but we give them no more weight than they deserve. Could you even *thank* God when you find your heart returning more than you wish to such thoughts, such "noisy quarrelling"? Thank him that your struggles with these burdensome thoughts help you remain humble and, therefore, closer to God, and ask him to use them to make you more understanding and patient toward others. "Say to him, 'It was good for me to be afflicted, that I might learn your statutes.'"

"As regards your interactions with others, express your reasons peacefully and with gentleness, and do not let yourself be disturbed." These words were written to a woman living in a difficult situation. In today's world there is so much heartache, so much division, so many who seem to be impossible to reach. Express your point of view with peace, with gentleness. Then let your heart trouble no further.

74. *Do not be surprised at your lack of energy, listlessness, and boredom in spiritual things; this is caused by age and physical issues. God does not exempt you from these, because ultimately, it is he himself who procures this for you, and he would be asking something impossible of you. He asks only that you be patient with yourself, that you always begin with a holy tenacity to be faithful in your spiritual practices. It is enough for him that you approve in your heart what those books say, and he accepts that approval just as if you had expressed those sentiments from the bottom of your heart. You must, therefore, be content with this as well. Otherwise we are not seeking to please God but rather to please ourselves. On the contrary, we should always seek above all what God wants rather than what we want, to have no hope in ourselves but rather in God, to adhere only to the holy and adorable will of God, and to hope only in his infinite mercy.*

I love the realism of these words, and I can imagine how healing they must have been to this woman who loved the Lord but felt the weight of her years and physical burdens. "Do not be surprised at your lack of energy, listlessness, and boredom in spiritual things; this is caused by age and physical issues." Do not be surprised or ashamed when you try to pray, to dedicate yourself to the things of God, and find yourself with no energy for these things, listless, even bored. Age and physical struggles are sometimes the cause. "God asks only that you be patient with yourself, that you always begin with a holy tenacity to be faithful in your spiritual practices." Again and again, be patient with yourself, be patient with your humanity. Just begin again. With a holy tenacity. With fidelity. This is all God asks.

Do you want to feel the sentiments you find in the Scripture passage you are reading, the mystery of the Rosary you are reciting, the part of the Liturgy of the Hours you are praying? And do you find yourself unable to do so? That desire is enough for God. For God, that sincere desire is as precious "as if you had expressed those sentiments from the bottom of your heart."

What matters, finally, even with regard to age and physical issues and how these affect your spiritual life, is what God wants—that is, always "to seek above all what God wants rather than what we want," always "to adhere only to the holy and adorable will of God," and always "to hope only in his infinite mercy." Hope. Mercy. Never discouragement.

75. *Let us also fix our gaze of faith on the Crucifix, and we will find that he was not satisfied only with the possibility of suffering but wished truly to suffer every kind of pain in body and in spirit, because it is not the mere possibility of suffering but suffering itself that brings us merit. Let us, then, accept from his hand every occasion of suffering and of practicing virtue. And because everything is disposed for our salvation, let us seek to enter his loving purpose and to adhere to it as best we can, sure that with every event and*

with every cross he gives his grace, and that each grace to which we adhere will have its eternal reward.

When I was provincial superior in my religious community, one year I visited our priests in Latin America. I had to make decisions that would affect the future of our mission there, and I did not have the answers. After lunch one day, I went out walking. As I walked, I reached the cathedral of this city. The cathedral was closed, but someone saw me at the door, and let me in. Alone in the cathedral, in the quiet of early afternoon, I walked the interior circuit of this enormous building. A severe earthquake had damaged it not long before, and the signs of the trauma were everywhere: cracks in the paint, broken statues, and similar.

I completed the circuit and stood before the altar. Then I looked up. Above me was the one undamaged work of art. Suspended from the ceiling was a large and beautiful cross, spared perhaps because it could sway with the tremors. As I looked, I thought of the ancient saying, *Stat crux, dum volvitur orbis* (When all else in the world is shaken and passes, the Cross stands firm). The Cross of Christ is the solid ground on which we can stand in time of suffering.

"Let us fix our gaze of faith on the Crucifix." Do you have a crucifix at hand? On your wall? Do you ever "fix your gaze" on it? Place a crucifix where you can see it. Frequently, and especially in times of suffering, fix your gaze of faith on the Crucifix. There you will see every kind of bodily pain—head, face, back, feet, hands—and every kind of emotional pain—isolation, abandonment, betrayal, unjust condemnation, ingratitude. Where you are, he has been. He understands. He shares your pain with you. "Let us, then, accept from his hand every occasion of suffering and of practicing virtue."

These words were written by a man himself long familiar with many kinds of bodily and emotional pain: the death of his mother when he was four, the deaths also of his father and six siblings by the time he was twenty-five, a share in the persecution of the Church, unjust condemnation, exile, damaged eyesight, breathing troubles, a fistula in the arm, gastrointestinal burdens as he aged. Venerable Bruno's life was described by a friend as a "long and painful career." Long and painful. When he counsels us to "fix our gaze of faith on the Crucifix," Venerable Bruno invites us to share his own practice, the practice that enabled him to bear his cross with faith, hope, a basic peace, and a heart open to others.

"Because everything is disposed for our salvation, let us seek to enter his loving purpose and to adhere to it as best we can." Both bodily and emotional pain. As best we can. That is all God asks.

And be "sure that with every event and with every cross he gives his grace, and that each grace to which we adhere will have its eternal reward." God will give you the grace you need to carry your cross—*be sure of this*. Remember, too, the eternal reward that awaits you when you carry that cross day by day.

76. *All that will happen to me, whether favorable or unfavorable, is prepared for me by God as an occasion of gain, may he be ever praised; I desire to profit from it.*

At one point, when physical burdens grew heavy, I taped these words to the door of my room. I wanted to see them often, every time I entered my room. I'm not sure how fully I lived them! I would have given anything to be free of the physical problems and for life to resume its normal course. But these words did help me find meaning in the burdens, to see in them "an occasion of gain." When eventually I wrote the biography of Venerable Bruno, I placed these words at the head of one of the chapters.

"All that will happen to me." *All*.

What is God asking you to carry now? What is happening to you now? What is favorable? Unfavorable? Can you try to say, with Venerable Bruno, that all this "is prepared for me by God as an occasion of gain, may he be ever praised; I desire to profit from it"?

> 77. *Anxieties, temptations, aridity, heaviness of heart, tribulations, injuries, unpleasant situations, offenses, ingratitude, crosses, matters which do not go well, and sorrows of various kinds: I will expect all these, even from those I love and whom I have helped. But I will never consider these as evil nor will I regard their origin in men, but rather in God. I know that nothing can take place against the will of God. I know that this is the way he himself followed here on earth and through which he led the saints closest to him, even his very Mother, so as to glorify her correspondingly in heaven. And so I will consider these as favors and opportunities that he gives me, so that I will need to ask his help, so that I will know my weakness, and do penance for my sins. I will try to accept them, confident that this is the road he has laid out for me, that all is ordered for my good, and that my part is to seek to benefit from these situations.*

Venerable Bruno included these counsels, too, in the spiritual program for a married woman. He speaks in her voice, giving her words to ponder and assimilate.

The list of crosses is detailed: anxieties, tribulations, injuries, ingratitude, sorrows of all kinds. And she may, Bruno tells her, receive such troubles "even from those I love and whom I have helped."

Venerable Bruno does not view this reality, however, simply on the human level: "I know that nothing can take place against the will of God. I know that this is the way he himself followed here on earth and through which he led the saints closest to him, even his very Mother." This path leads to a corresponding glory in heaven.

"And so I will consider these as favors and opportunities that he gives me." *Favors and opportunities*. I find that I cannot quickly pass by these words. They call for a kind of "daily heroism," what Pope Francis calls "the middle-class of holiness" (*Apostolic Exhortation on the Call to Holiness in Today's World*, 7) — a holiness, a heroism, that all can live in daily life. I think, for example, of St. Thérèse, who strove to love especially those whom she found most difficult.

Venerable Bruno asks us to view such relationships and such situations with faith. Three benefits follow: In these situations, we learn our need for God's help; we experience our weakness, especially our struggle to love, and so become humbler, gentler with others, and more understanding; and we do penance for our own faults and sins.

Venerable Bruno's conclusion follows: "I will try to accept them, confident that this is the road he has laid out for me, that all is ordered for my good, and that my part is to seek to benefit from these situations."

78. *Keep your eyes on the Crucifix, to which we must conform ourselves, remembering as you do this that Jesus Crucified is not only our model but also our help and our reward.*

Pope Francis tells us, "Here is the key to our salvation, the key for having patience on the journey of life, the key to overcoming our deserts: looking at the Crucifix" (March 20, 2018). And again: "Let us think deeply about the suffering of Jesus, and let us say to ourselves: This is for my sake. Even if I had been the only person in the world, he would have done it. He did it for me. Let us kiss the Crucifix and say, 'For my sake. Thank you, Jesus. For me'" (April 16, 2014).

When suffering enters your life, "keep your eyes on the Crucifix." There you find a model of perseverance, a help in your pain, and a reward for your faithfulness. There, too, you know that you are loved.

> 79. *I will treat all with gentleness, and this will be the subject of my particular examination.*

The effort to be gentle, patient, and warm with others did not, I believe, come easily to Venerable Bruno; it was a lifelong endeavor. "Particular examination" is a phrase of St. Ignatius. It indicates an area of special spiritual need to which particular attention is given in the search for growth. For Venerable Bruno, this was to treat others with warmness, kindness, and understanding—with the gentleness of Jesus (Matt. 11:29).

Is Jesus also calling you to grow in this? If not in this, in what other part of the spiritual life?

> 80. *For my particular examination on gentleness, I will read in Rodriguez or elsewhere about the nature, kinds, acts, degrees, aids, obstacles, means, and examples of this virtue; from time to time, I will compare my response to others with the way Jesus Christ responds to those he meets; immediately upon arising, I will renew my proposal to grow in this virtue and will ask God's help; I will examine myself often on this virtue and note my failures in writing, even when walking through the streets; before going to bed I will make my particular examination on this and review my progress day by day and week by week.*

Venerable Bruno continues the preceding quote. These words reveal how diligently he pursued the gentleness of Jesus. He put his heart into this effort! A year before his death, a man making a retreat under Venerable Bruno's guidance wrote to his wife, "For myself, I can tell you that I am very happy with Father Lanteri. I have spent much time with him. I find him gentle, persuasive, and, above all, most considerate. God gives him much light to understand and explain things very well." And in another letter, "The superior, Father Lanteri, is very gentle." Venerable Bruno's long, tireless efforts bore fruit.

He begins with spiritual reading to nourish this effort. The "Rodriguez" he mentions is Alonso Rodriguez, S.J., and his classic work, *The Practice of Christian Perfection.* Here Venerable Bruno learns about the nature of Christ's gentleness, various kinds of gentleness, different acts of gentleness, successive degrees of this virtue, obstacles that impede it, the means to grow in it, and examples of people who practiced it. A thorough grounding! Increasingly, Bruno perceives the path to growth in this virtue.

Periodically, Venerable Bruno will compare his way of responding to others with the way Jesus responds to those he meets: Jesus's sensitivity to their needs, his listening, the encouragement he gives them, the new hope he inspires in them.

Upon rising in the morning, Venerable Bruno will renew his proposal to treat others with Jesus's own gentleness, asking Jesus's help. Throughout the day, he will review his interactions and note any failures in writing. Before retiring, he will examine the day in this regard. Day by day, week by week, Venerable Bruno will review his progress.

Is it any wonder that he grew in the gentleness of Christ, and so became a source of such hope and encouragement to many?

Where is God calling you to grow? Can you plan concretely, with the Lord, how to proceed? Venerable Bruno's example reveals that such efforts, well organized and directed, made with God's grace, and faithfully pursued through the years, bear more fruit than we can imagine.

81. *When I learned from your mother-in-law that you had lost your little Enrico, I felt great sorrow for what you must be*

undergoing, because no sacrifice could be more painful for you. He had such wonderful qualities that he won the love of all, and how much more the love of his mother. And so, because of this, you have every reason to feel his loss and to weep for him.

Venerable Bruno writes to a woman he was guiding spiritually, Gabriella, a wife and mother of six children. He has just learned that Gabriella's little son Enrico has died and hastens to write to her. Already Gabriella had lost two sons. The death now of a third will pierce her heart. Venerable Bruno knows this and so writes immediately.

When I share Venerable Bruno's writings, often this letter above all speaks to the listeners' hearts. One woman whose teenage son died defending the life of another wrote, "This letter is easily the most consoling message I have received on the journey." It must have meant much also to Gabriella, who kept it all her life. After her death, her daughter-in-law found it among her papers.

The words cited here give the opening lines of Venerable Bruno's letter. Before all else, he validates Gabriella's human sorrow, the pain her mother's heart feels. There are no recriminations, no reproof, no words to the effect of, "You know that he is with God, and so you should not feel sorrow, you should not weep." Venerable Bruno himself feels "great sorrow," and affirms that "no sacrifice could be more painful for you," and that "you have every reason to feel his loss and to weep for him." When Jesus sees Mary weep at the death of her brother, he, too, weeps and is not ashamed of those tears (John 11:33–35).

82. *Yet, in another way, I share with you a joy that you have surely gained a protector in heaven who cannot fail to care for you, because he is your son. And because you love him so deeply, turn your thoughts to his eternal happiness, share*

in his glory, and do not imagine that you have lost him. It would be wrong to think so, because you have lost him only from sight, and not in reality. Consider that he is at your side like another angel, that he encourages you to dedicate yourself to the things of heaven, and to share in his joy; that he assures you of his efforts before the throne of the Most Holy Trinity for you, for his father, his brother, and his dear sisters, to obtain for all of you great and abundant graces for your eternal salvation.

Venerable Bruno does not remain only on the human level. He raises Gabriella's heart now to the level of faith: "Yet, in another way, I share with you a joy that you have surely gained a protector in heaven who cannot fail to care for you, because he is your son."

The bond of mother and son remains, Bruno reminds the grieving Gabriella: "And because you love him so deeply, turn your thoughts to his eternal happiness, share in his glory, and do not imagine that you have lost him. It would be wrong to think so, because you have lost him only from sight, and not in reality. Consider that he is at your side like another angel." As your guardian angel accompanies you constantly, so, too, now, does Enrico.

"Consider ... that he encourages you to dedicate yourself to the things of heaven, and to share in his joy; that he assures you of his efforts before the throne of the Most Holy Trinity for you, for his father, his brother, and his dear sisters, to obtain for all of you great and abundant graces for your eternal salvation." He is with you; he loves you; he brings your needs and those of everyone dear to you before God, interceding on behalf of the family.

83. *Remain in continual and loving conversation with Enrico. Speak to him about all that you experience in your own heart, all that happens in your family, and anything of importance for you.*

OVERCOMING SPIRITUAL DISCOURAGEMENT

This is the teaching of the communion of saints in practice, a communion that is real, that can be lived. "Remain in continual and loving *conversation* with him." Gabriella can speak with Enrico about her life and all that she loves, and he can understand better than ever before.

> 84. *Be on guard against thinking that he does not care about you, or that he is powerless to help you. That would be a misunderstanding of the immense love and almost infinite power that each of the Blessed enjoys, with all the other divine perfections that God shares with them in the greatest possible abundance.*

The "almost infinite power that each of the Blessed enjoys." What a beautiful and striking concept! I think of these words when I ask the intercession of my own parents and others who, I am confident, are with the Lord. Venerable Bruno assures Gabriella that she has a powerful intercessor before God, one who loves her deeply.

> 85. *And so, if before you had no reason to be discouraged in the service of God, you have much less reason now. I would add that if it were possible for your little Enrico to feel any sorrow even now in heaven, it would be to see you discouraged and saddened because of him, because of your own failings, or because of the difficulties you encounter in the service of God. This will be the remedy for any sadness or lack of courage you may feel: the thought that, with the grace of God and the protection of your little Enrico, you can do all things.*

These final words must have meant much to Gabriella. Here, Venerable Bruno's trademark gentle but insistent call to resist discouragement acquires a new aspect, now applied to a grieving mother: "This will be the remedy for any sadness or lack of courage you may feel: the thought that, with the grace of God and the protection of your little Enrico, you can do all things."

If sadness for the loss of a loved one burdens your heart, take time to read Venerable Bruno's letter to this sorrowing mother. Let these truths of faith bring light and strength to your heart. Let the Blessed in heaven bring you encouragement, joined with you, walking with you, sharing life with you, in the communion of saints.

"Behold, God's dwelling is with the human race. He will dwell with them, and they will be his people, and God himself will always be with them [as their God]. He will wipe every tear from their eyes, and there shall be no more death or mourning, wailing or pain, [for] the old order has passed away" (Rev. 21:3–4).

86. *If you want peace in this life, you must, first of all, decide to accommodate yourself to circumstances and not demand that circumstances accommodate themselves to you. You must, secondly, strive to practice uniformity of your will with God's. It is he who disposes everything, arranges everything, and permits all that takes place. We need only seek and follow the plan of his fatherly love for our lives, which is always to provide us opportunities for practicing different virtues, at times one, at times another, so that he will have something for which to reward us.*

"If you want peace in this life," love, pray, give, and serve in your present circumstances, not waiting for a more opportune time that may never come. This is St. John Paul II's Law of the Gift: As long as I seek happiness by insisting on my way, my time, my projects, my plans, I will never be happy; but when I give of myself in love and service to God and others, a wonderful thing happens — I become happy.

OVERCOMING SPIRITUAL DISCOURAGEMENT

Blessed Solanus Casey counsels, "Do not pray for easy lives, pray to be stronger. Do not pray for tasks equal to your powers, pray for powers equal to your tasks. Then the doing of your work shall be no miracle, but you shall be a miracle. Every day you shall wonder at yourself, at the richness of life that has come to you by the grace of God" (cited by a witness in the cause of canonization).

87. *I have noticed in your letters that you often turn in on yourself. Try to watch for this and to focus less often on yourself, but to serve God with great simplicity. Instead of turning in on yourself, lift your gaze often with peace and love to God, to his lovable will, to his adorable Providence. Tell him that regardless of whether you do well or poorly, you want to be totally his, and that it is his to make you become better. Cast also upon him all your concerns about your children and your husband. The more you trust in him, the greater will be his care for you.*

Do you find yourself turning inward, preoccupied by your anxieties and burdened by your failings? "Instead of turning in on yourself, lift your gaze often with peace and love to God." Often. With peace. With love. The less you focus on your failures and the more you gaze on the Lord with peace and love, the more your heart will lift, the stronger you will become, the more joy you will find. Tell him that "you want to be totally his," and, with boldness, tell him that "it is *his* to make you become better"!

Are you concerned about many things? "Cast also upon him all your concerns," for "the more you trust in him, the greater will be his care for you."

Venerable Bruno most likely recalls here the words of Scripture, "Cast all your worries upon him because he cares for you" (1 Pet. 5:7). What worries fill your heart today? Cast them upon the Lord with trust.

88. *"Paradise pays for all."*

These were the words of Father Nikolaus von Diessbach, a saintly man and spiritual director of Venerable Bruno for twenty years. Venerable Bruno heard Father Diessbach repeat them and, in his own sufferings, often quoted them. From time to time, I think of this sentence. Four little words that express a deep, fundamental truth: When borne with Jesus, our sorrows, heartaches, and pains are not empty suffering; they will be repaid and with overflowing measure. Yes, paradise — an eternity of joy with God and those we love in the communion of the saints — gives meaning to all our sorrows. Venerable Bruno repeated these words in times of physical pain and limitation, when, for example, his ailments left him nearly unable to breathe. On such occasions, the thought of eternal life with God strengthened him to persevere. "Paradise pays for all."

89. *Thursday at 9:00 a.m., a few words in a hurry. I received your letter and mother's. I have a chance now to reply, and am sending you what I had already written. . . . I was deeply moved when I received your letter. I had gone to Father Lanteri to ask permission to read it. I found him physically worse than the other days. He said, "Read as much as you wish; the sentiments of the heart are pleasing to God." But tears were falling from his eyes, he could scarcely breathe. "The lamp is going out," he said. His whole being was at peace. He looks to heaven during his attacks and pronounces the word "paradise" with so much faith that it stirs everything within me. . . . It is sweet, my Adèle, to shed such tears. I shed many at these words.*

Words of the retreatant cited earlier, from another letter to his wife. One year before Venerable Bruno's death, he guided this man's retreat. Careful not to break the seclusion of the retreat, the man asks Bruno if it is fitting that he read his wife's letter. "He said, 'Read as much as you wish; the sentiments of the heart are pleasing to God.'" The love of husband and wife, so pleasing to God, will not distract from the retreat.

Here it is best to slow the pace and simply witness the peace and faith with which Venerable Bruno faces his physical weakness, knowing that the end approaches.

Bruno repeats, "Paradise pays for all." Say these words. Again.

The thought of eternal life lifts his heart: "He pronounces the word 'paradise' with so much faith that to hear it moves everything within me." Hear him say that word. Feel all that it means for him—and for you.

If we live the Cross with Jesus, with him we will live the resurrection as well.

Chapter Five

LIVING WITH MARY

90. He loved the Virgin Mary deeply.

This and the following quotations are from a paragraph written by Oblate Father Antonio Ferrero, one of the first Oblates and Venerable Bruno's confessor in his last months. The Oblates had asked Father Giovanni Battista Rubino (a future Servant of God) to preach at a Mass celebrated in commemoration of Venerable Bruno thirty days after his death. Father Ferrero supplied Father Rubino with the information he needed for his sermon. In doing so, Father Ferrero, a personal witness, left us a rich description of Venerable Bruno's life and spirit. In the paragraph we will now explore, Father Ferrero speaks of Bruno's relationship with Mary.

I have translated this first sentence as, "He loved the Virgin Mary deeply." The original reads, *Era innamorato di Maria Vergine.* In Italian, when a person falls in love, he or she is said to be *innamorato* or *innamorata.* Most literally, the translation would read, "He was in love with the Virgin Mary" — that is, he loved her deeply, she was the love of his life, she was his "Lady," as he described her in another text.

Mary was there when Bruno lost his mother, Margherita, at age four. From that time, Mary was the feminine, maternal presence in his life. She was there at the end of his life, comforting him in a special way as his earthly life drew to a close. And Mary was there every step of the way through the years of Venerable Bruno's "long and painful career." She was the tenderness, the warmth, and the love that eased burdens, gave new energy, and instilled hope.

"He loved the Virgin Mary deeply." What better can we do—we who also live in difficult times, who also need a loving, tender, warm, spiritual presence—than to love Mary deeply, than to fall in love with her?

91. He surrounded himself with images of her.

As my mother's many grandchildren were born and grew, she placed their photos on the refrigerator door where she would see them often. When I enter a home and see refrigerators, counters, or desks that display photos of loved ones, my heart lifts. These people are dear to those who surround themselves with their photos and who want often to be reminded of them.

Venerable Bruno related to Mary in the same way. If you visited his apartment or any place where he lived, you would always find images, paintings, and statutes of Mary. Bruno wished to live with visual reminders of Mary so that she would never be far from his awareness as the day unfolded.

Several images of Mary are special to me. One I have on my wall, Our Lady of Consolation, from her shrine in Turin, Italy. Another I keep in my breviary, an image of Our Lady of Guadalupe. For my computer desktop and as wallpaper for my phone, I have chosen the icon of Our Lady of Tenderness. These images remind me of Mary every day, and often during the day.

Do you have images of Mary around you? Could such images help you to remember and to turn to her tenderness and love during the day?

92. He kept a precious collection of books that speak of her and read from them for a few hours every week.

Living with Mary

If you look at a person's bookshelf, you quickly perceive his or her interests. It might be gardening, golf, history, literature, or politics. If you looked at Venerable Bruno's bookshelves, you would conclude that he took great interest in Mary. You would see books about the Church's teaching on Mary, her place in the spiritual life, the history of Marian devotion, and so on. You would encounter St. Alphonsus Liguori's *The Glories of Mary*, Jesuit Jean Crasset's *Devotion to Mary*, Father Alexandre-Joseph Derouville's *The Imitation of Mary*, and many others.

If you read about a subject for one or two hours a week, week after week, year after year, what happens? Obviously, you become deeply familiar with that subject. Your knowledge of it grows as reading builds on reading. The subject is never far from your consciousness, and your appreciation of it develops, amplified by the steady nourishment you receive through this reading.

What happened, then, to Venerable Bruno's devotion to Mary as he read so consistently and devotedly about her? That relationship never grew stale, never remained static. It was always young, fresh, new, expanding, alive. When he turned to Mary, prayed to her, and thought of her, further insights fed that relationship. It is said that we can only love what we know. As his knowledge of Mary grew, Venerable Bruno's love for her did likewise.

Do you read about Mary? Listen to podcasts about her? How might it be possible for you to deepen your knowledge and love of her? Can you choose one concrete way of doing this? Today, printed and digital resources abound. Choose one. Begin.

93. He celebrated her novenas.

In his writings, we see Venerable Bruno begin nine days before the feast of the Assumption to pray and prepare for that feast. He did the same for other Marian feasts as well, such as the Immaculate Conception.

How do we celebrate Our Lady's Assumption when we think of it on that day? Certainly, Mass and whatever commemoration we make will be fruitful, and grace will come through this. But what if we prepared for several days, pondering the meaning of the feast and praying that the day bring us grace, awaken fresh desire for eternal life, and lead us closer to Mary and so to Jesus? The Assumption of Mary would have a deeper and richer impact. This was Venerable Bruno's desire: to benefit fully from the Marian celebrations in the liturgical year.

Can these celebrations become more grace-filled for you? Is there a way of preparing that might help? A way of living them?

94. *He spoke very often about her.*

The original word is *frequentissimamente*, the superlative of the adverb. It is the strongest way of saying "very often." It indicates that you could not be in Bruno's company for long without hearing some reference to Mary.

Ex abundantia cordis, os loquitur. "Out of the abundance of the heart the mouth speaks" (Matt. 12:34, RSVCE). I once lived with a man whose conversation, wherever it began, always turned to the place where he grew up. He loved that place, and it was so present to his heart that his words frequently turned to it. From the abundance of the heart, the mouth speaks: We speak most often of what we love most.

For this reason, Venerable Bruno spoke very often about Mary. She was so dear to his heart, so present to him, that *frequentissimamente*, often, readily, with unforced naturalness, and because he loved her so deeply, he spoke of her.

Do you ever speak of Mary? "From the abundance of the heart, the mouth speaks." Just fall more and more in love with her, and the words will come—words that will be welcome to others and a blessing for you and for them.

95. *He said that it was not enough simply to inspire devotion for her in others, but that it was necessary to lead them to a great confidence in her.*

"To a great confidence." This confidence is so blessed. Several times in my life, I have been in situations that I thought desperate, beyond resolution. In such times, my heart turns spontaneously to Mary, confident that, as the classic prayer says, "Never was it known that anyone who fled to your protection, implored your help, or sought your intercession was left unaided." Never. I have always found that prayer true.

Two memories come to my heart. One is the farewell talk that Monsignor Ronald Knox gave to the Oxford students he served as chaplain. As they were about to leave the university, he asked them to remember two things: that whatever might happen in their lives, they should never hesitate to turn to Jesus for mercy and healing; and that in whatever problems they might find themselves, they could always turn to Mary. She would never, he told them, let them down.

Once I was alone in a church. I looked at the stained-glass windows and realized that each depicted some title of Mary. I grew interested and looked at them all, one by one. The final window was Our Lady of Hope. I stayed there, gazing at the window, absorbing the meaning of the image and the title. Our Lady of Hope. She does give us hope, and she can do so for you. The more you turn to Mary in times of need, the more you will experience the truth "that never was it known that anyone who fled to your protection, implored your help, or sought your intercession was left unaided."

96. *He spoke of her as his mother, as the one who nurtured him, and as his paradise.*

These were three ways in which Venerable Bruno thought of and related to Mary. She was his mother, the one who eased the pain of his earthly mother's death when he was four, who became the maternal presence in his life. Father Ferrero testified that one day Bruno told him, "I have hardly known any other mother than the Virgin Mary, and in all my life, I have never received anything but caresses from so good a mother."

Mary is, the Second Vatican Council tells us, "our mother in the order of grace" (*Constitution on the Church*, 61) — that is, the maternal presence of love and tenderness that accompanies us in all that concerns the spiritual life: our relationship with God, our prayer, the daily living of our respective vocations, our hope of eternal life.

I think of Mary as mother in this way: Two children come home from school. In one home, the mother is there; in the other, she is away. In both cases, the children play, study, eat, and do all the rest. But so much is different when the mother is there — a warmth, a security, a love. That is the difference Mary makes in our spiritual lives.

Venerable Bruno thought of Mary as the one who nurtured him. The Italian word used refers specifically to the care of a young infant in the first year or two of life, watched over and attended to in its needs.

And she was "his paradise" — the one in whose presence the sorrows of life diminished, in whose love he found peace and joy.

Oblate Brother Pietro Gardetti, who assisted Venerable Bruno in his last weeks, recounts, "One evening, as dusk was falling, we were saying the Rosary together. He was seated on his small chair, and I was next to him, kneeling on the floor. He interrupted me, and asked me who that Lady was who had come to visit them. I replied that I had not seen any Lady, because this was a cloistered area. Then we resumed the rosary to its end." And Father Ferrero relates, "In his last illness, he told me several times that he had a beautiful Lady with a lovely child in her arms who never left him, but would say no more." His mother, the one who nurtured him, his paradise.

Venerable Bruno invites you, too, to turn to Mary with the same love and confidence.

> 97. *Let all those into whose hands this document may fall know that I, the undersigned Pio Bruno Lanteri, offer myself as perpetual slave of the Blessed Virgin Mary, our Lady, with an unconditional, free, and perfect gift of my person and all my possessions, that she may dispose of them according to her good pleasure as my true and absolute Lady.*

Venerable Bruno made his act of consecration to Mary at age twenty-two, as his priestly ordination drew near. He kept this handwritten page all his life and lived the consecration it expresses. His text means much to me, as I used it thirty-eight years ago to make a similar consecration. I am sure that I have not lived it as richly as Venerable Bruno! But it retains a warm place in my spiritual life and remains a source of grace. I keep the page on which I wrote this text in my breviary and am looking at it now as I write.

At a given point in our lives, we may consecrate ourselves to Jesus through Mary. As the years pass, we may not always remember that we have done this. From time to time, we do. But Mary never forgets, and the relationship strengthened through this consecration continues to bless us.

What place does consecration to Mary have in your life? What place might it have?

> 98. *I desire to have a tender love for the Virgin Mary, and a confidence in her as a son toward his mother, to such a degree that it appear impossible to me that she could permit me to be overcome and that I be lost in the battle; I will have recourse to her, therefore, as the chick takes refuge under the wings of*

its mother when it hears the cries of the preying hawk, and, after the act of the love of God, I shall say, Monstra te esse matrem, Sub tuum praesidium, Maria mater gratiae, etc., and I will do this with the confidence that a child has toward its mother, asking of her what it needs with great surety, as if she were bound to grant it to him, and turning to her in all his troubles, such that the mother is, as it were, obliged to come to his aid, and draws from this a motive to love her son yet more deeply. And if earthly mothers, though at times they may not be good, do not refuse the requests of their children, what shall be said of the great Mother of God?

These are words from Bruno's personal spiritual program composed shortly before ordination and conserved throughout his life. He desires to have "a tender love for the Virgin Mary, and a confidence in her as a son toward his mother." He, and we, can turn to her in any danger. The Latin texts Venerable Bruno cites are classic prayers, beautiful prayers and loved through the centuries: Hail Star of the Sea; We Fly to Thy Patronage; Mary, Mother of Grace.

"I desire to have a tender love for the Virgin Mary." May God grant all of us that desire and that reality.

Chapter Six

LIVING WITH COURAGE

99. *Therefore, be of good courage. Let your heart be joyful, give yourself as completely as you can to God, banish any doubts, and tell God that you never wish consciously to do anything that would displease him. For the rest, do not be troubled. God is with you and will help you and will not let you fall.*

"Be of good courage." Here Venerable Bruno highlights the virtue of fortitude, one of the four cardinal virtues. The *Catechism of the Catholic Church* describes fortitude as "the moral virtue that ensures firmness in difficulties and constancy in the pursuit of the good." Fortitude helps us, the *Catechism* continues, to "strengthen the resolve to resist temptations" and "to overcome obstacles in the moral life." It "enables one to conquer fear" and "to face trials and persecutions" (1808). The gift of the Holy Spirit by this same name, the gift of fortitude, empowers us to do all this with energy and greater ease. We can think of saints like St. Thomas More, more recently St. Edith Stein and St. Maximilian Kolbe, and so many others, known and unknown. The virtue and gift of fortitude gave them strength to follow the Lord faithfully when courage was needed. Fortitude was evident also in the life of Venerable Bruno, especially in his steadfastness in times of trial. This virtue and this gift are yours as well, poured into your heart in your Baptism and Confirmation.

"Therefore, be of good courage!" Venerable Bruno speaks these words to you today — you who, like him, live in difficult times. Further, he says, "Let your heart be joyful, give yourself as completely as you can to God, banish any doubts, and tell God that you never wish consciously to do anything that would displease him." And then, "For the rest, do not be troubled. God is with you and will help you and will not let you fall."

100. *Be persistent in constantly renewing, even daily, and several times a day, your proposals, even if they are always the same and even if you fulfill them very poorly, because in this way you exclude at least the will to continue in your failings; it is precisely this that the Lord desires of you and in which the holiness of which we are capable in this life consists. This holiness consists not in no longer failing, but in not persevering in the will to fail. On the contrary, this very persistence in always beginning has something heroic about it.*

This was written to a woman who loved the Lord, who was living in a difficult situation, and who was discouraged. Venerable Bruno never ceases to call us out of discouragement! Persist, continue, do not give up, do not give in. Even if your efforts seem so poor, this refusal to surrender, this willingness to persist, is all God asks: "It is precisely this that the Lord desires of you and in which the holiness of which we are capable in this life consists."

"This holiness consists not in no longer failing, but in not persevering in the will to fail." You will give in to impatience, lack of charity, and other failings. But this does not impede your quest for holiness. Just begin again each time, and you are solidly on the path to sanctity.

"On the contrary, this very persistence in always beginning has something heroic about it." *Something heroic.* Venerable Bruno turns the tables on discouragement: What appeared to be the end of progress in the spiritual life—the cycle of failure and beginning again—is actually a heroic step toward holiness. This heroism is available to us all.

> 101. *Concretely, then, always be very sure that you will fail many times a day, but be constant nonetheless in rising again immediately every time, and thus you will practice humility and firm confidence in God, virtues we need to progress greatly in the service of God. Persevere in your commitment to doing things without impetuosity, and you will gain fruit from them; it will not be the fruit of your diligence but of God's blessing, who will reward your diligence, and this certainly if you do so with perseverance.*

These are further words to the same woman, but they are for us all. Who of us does not know the experience of repeated failures, even "many times a day"? Venerable Bruno's call is ever the same: "Be constant nonetheless in rising again immediately every time." Begin again. Immediately. Every time. If we do this we will grow humbler, have more trust in the Lord, and "progress greatly in the service of God."

"Persevere in your commitment to doing things without impetuosity, and you will gain fruit from them." Without impetuosity, without strain, without exhausting efforts—with intention, with faith, with love. God does not ask that we drive ourselves to exhaustion. "The fruit of the Spirit is love, joy, peace, patience, kindness, generosity, faithfulness, gentleness, self-control" (Gal. 5:22–23). Persevere, and your efforts will bear fruit, a work of God's grace in you.

102. I, of myself, can do nothing good, but I can do all things in God who is so lovingly concerned for my salvation that he will never fail me with his grace.

"I can do all things in him who strengthens me" (Phil. 4:13, RS-VCE). "Nothing will be impossible for God" (Luke 1:37). Venerable Bruno recognizes two truths: "Of myself, I can do nothing good." "I can do all things in God," in God "who is so lovingly concerned for my salvation that he will never fail me with his grace."

These two truths apply to us as well. Deep internalization of them leads to a double spiritual richness: a humble sense of self (Matt. 5:3) and an unshakeable confidence in God's personal love for us. This double awareness is the root of Mary's joyful song, "My spirit rejoices in God my savior. For he has looked upon his handmaid's lowliness" (Luke 1:47–48).

103. I propose today to think, speak, and act as would a saint, and to practice acts of generosity: God, come to my assistance. To you I direct all my abilities and all my actions.

As the day begins, Venerable Bruno looks to the saints and does not hesitate to seek their love of God — to think, to speak, and to act as they do, to be generous and great-hearted in serving God.

The Second Vatican Council spoke of the universal call to holiness. We know this, and we assent to it. Do we dare to hope for it? Do you dare? Concretely? Can you say, with Venerable Bruno, as the day begins, "I propose today to think, speak, and act as would a saint," and ask, "God, come to my assistance," in the genuine hope that this may truly happen?

I had just celebrated the funeral of a wonderful woman who died in her eighties. Her children, grandchildren, and great-grandchildren were present in the packed church. She had lived a faithful life of prayer and loving service to her family and to many others. After the Mass, I spoke with a man who commented, "This is another of those saints who will never be canonized." That is what you and I, too, are called to be: saints. It begins with the daily commitment to seek sanctity.

> 104. *Let your heart be in peace and have courage, because Jesus, your Spouse, desires that you be a saint, but, let it be understood, a saint with defects, not without defects. Be sure that God is more pleased with weak but humble virtue than with strong virtue, but proud.*

This is from a letter to a religious sister whose community had been closed under the French occupation. After Napoleon's defeat, she reentered religious life in a community that had survived. The transition was difficult.

Again, discouragement; again the call to peace of heart, to courage, and to be a saint: "Jesus … desires that you be a saint, but, let it be understood, a saint with defects, not without defects." A saint, *but a saint with defects*, and not without them. This is real. This is the sanctity to which we are all called. This is possible!

And then a note: "Be sure that God is more pleased with weak but humble virtue than with strong virtue, but proud." "Weak but humble virtue" and "strong virtue but proud": God loves the former.

One who knew him testified that many religious left their meetings with Venerable Bruno consoled in their sorrows. Here we meet one of them. That consolation is ours as well.

> 105. *Seek only to receive everything from the hand of God so as to merit all the more, and this itself will help to diminish your cross. Otherwise the cross becomes still more heavy and hard to bear. It is in our interest to make of*

necessity a virtue. I have proposed these all too human motives because our humanity needs all that can help to encourage us.

This, too, is from a letter to a woman in a difficult situation. Sister Leopolda Mortigliengo was born in Turin and entered the Visitation Sisters at age seventeen. After thirty-nine years of life in the monastery, she, too, was evicted from her convent by order of the French police. Sister Leopolda returned to her family, and a difficult time began for her. For the next fourteen years, until her death, she struggled to maintain what she could of her religious life while living at home. This quotation and the next two are taken from a letter Bruno wrote to her during those years.

Recognizing the difficulty of Sister Leopolda's circumstances, Venerable Bruno invites her to receive her struggles "from the hand of God." If she sees them only humanly, they will become harder yet to bear. "It is," he tells her, "in our interest to make of necessity a virtue. I have proposed these all too human motives because our humanity needs all that can help to encourage us." The perspective of faith lightens our struggles, something that even humanly we desire.

As so often, Venerable Bruno begins by affirming our human reality and then lifting it to the level of faith.

106. *I know that you also love noble and generous motives in your service of God, and this is very much as it should be because he is so great and merits all that we can give. Try to find strength for this effort with prayer made at chosen times in the day. Prepare the subject of your meditation, and follow the prescribed rules for doing it well. These are simple means that draw upon you the blessing of God. At the least, you will suffer less from distractions and dryness of voluntary origin. This will be the more true if you seek*

throughout the day to pay little heed to your castles in the
air because they serve only to torment you the more. This
is not easy, but you will only be happy in heaven, so that
it is best to accept the crosses the Lord sends us, because
these are always the most suited to us and are always ac-
companied by great graces.

Venerable Bruno knows, too, that this woman loves the Lord, that beyond the human considerations just mentioned, "you also love noble and generous motives in your service of God." Prayer will give her this strength, "prayer made at chosen times in the day," prayer that is prepared and made according to the rule of her religious life. Fidelity to your daily program of prayer, he tells her and us, will "draw upon you the blessing of God. At the least, you will suffer less from distractions and dryness of voluntary origin."

If she — and we — can avoid wishing that things were different, can avoid "castles in the air," then all this will indeed be easier. Jean-Pierre de Caussade, S.J., writes, "There is never a moment when God does not come forward in the guise of some suffering or some duty, and all that takes place within us, around us and through us both includes and hides his activity" (*Abandonment to Divine Providence*, II, 1).

Here, and in these circumstances, with these people, through these tasks, God comes to you and calls you to give of yourself in love and service.

107. *Be patient with yourself, bear with your faults with hu-*
mility and confidence in God. Do not forget the spirit of
interior renunciation and of gentleness toward others so
recommended by your holy father [St. Francis de Sales],
and the eternal joy prepared for you that will reward you
for all this.

Our hearts need to hear these invitations again and again: "Be patient with yourself," "bear your faults with humility and confidence"—again this pairing: a humble appraisal of our own strength and unlimited confidence in God's strength at work in us—"interior renunciation," "gentleness toward others" as modeled and taught by St. Francis de Sales, and the thought of "the eternal joy prepared for you that will reward you for all this."

St. Francis de Sales writes, "We must not only speak gently to our neighbor, but we must be filled, heart and soul with gentleness; and we must not merely seek the sweetness of aromatic honey in courtesy and suavity with strangers, but also the sweetness of milk among those of our own household and our neighbors" (*The Introduction to the Devout Life*, III, 8).

> 108. *The truths that have persuaded me are those that persuaded the saints. They are and will always be the same; neither time nor lack of reflection will make them lose their power; and therefore, just as they moved me once, so, with the help of God, they must always move me.*

On what do we base our lives? What guiding principles? What truths? Everything depends on this!

"The truths that have persuaded me are those that persuaded the saints." These are the solid, sure, foundational, and inspiring truths by which we, too, can live. What truths inspired St. Augustine? St. Thomas Aquinas? St. Francis of Assisi? St. Catherine of Siena? St. Ignatius of Loyola? St. Teresa of Avila? St. Teresa of Calcutta? St. John Paul II? They were not mistaken. Venerable Bruno chooses to live by those truths—and invites us to do the same.

These truths—that we are created by God, that we are called to love and serve him in the vocation he has given us, that we will find love and grace to do this through Jesus Christ, the Church, and the sacraments, and that we are called to an eternity of life with the Trinity—"are and will always be the same."

Bruno desires that these unchanging truths guide not only his youthful years but every stage of his life. "Neither time nor lack of reflection will make them lose their power; and therefore, just as they moved me once, so, with the help of God, they must always move me." And us as well. And you as well, in your present stage of life. This is a grace to ask of God, that these truths always retain their savor in our hearts!

109. *Do all with a great will, and even little things will have great value.*

Little things, like beginning the day, smiling at another person, preparing a meal, speaking on the phone, answering email, interacting with your husband, your wife, your children, doing your work—"Do all with a great will, and even little things will have great value."

I recently read the 281 letters of St. Zélie Martin, the mother of St. Thérèse of Lisieux. In Venerable Bruno's sense, her life was made of "little things"—her relationship with her husband, raising her five daughters, helping them in their struggles, managing the family lace-making business, interacting with her workers and clients, spending time in prayer and in church, helping others in need. As I read, I marveled at the love St. Zélie put into these daily "little things." She did them "with a great will," and they had "great value." The life of her daughter, St. Thérèse, was likewise composed of "little things," such as helping prepare for meals, attending to the sacristy, accompanying the novices, composing plays for the community's recreation—and Pope St. Pius X called her "the greatest saint of modern times."

"Do all with a great will, and even little things will have great value." This is our path—your path—to holiness. You can do this today.

110. *I do not live except for the glory of God; to this alone I must dedicate all my abilities of soul and body. And when it is necessary to think, speak, and labor for God, to give my very life, let all be lost, let whatever will happen, happen: This I must do.*

These were not just abstract words for Venerable Bruno. A time came when the pope was held captive by Napoleon, and Venerable Bruno knew that he put his life on the line in defending him. In fact, he was arrested, interrogated, stripped of his priestly ministry, and exiled—an exile he did not expect to survive.

What will our times ask of us as faithful followers of Jesus and members of the his Body, the Church? What did they ask of St. Thomas More? Of those who live their Christian faith in places and times of persecution? "When it is necessary to think, speak, and labor for God, to give my very life, let all be lost, let whatever will happen, happen: This I must do." With quiet trust in the Father's love, in the power of Jesus's saving grace, in the courage infused by the Holy Spirit, let this desire, this prayer, arise from your heart too.

111. *Any act of charity merits eternal life, and in the other life we will no longer be able to render service to God.*

"Seventy is the sum of our years, or eighty, if we are strong" (Ps. 90:10). Every one of these years is God's gift, a time to show love to him and to those he has placed in our lives: "Any act of charity merits eternal life."

"In the other life we will no longer be able to render service to God." Now, today, this week is the time to love and to serve. Each day offers us the "sacrament of the present moment," as Father Jean-Pierre de Caussade calls it, an opportunity to respond to God's call to love right now.

To what act of charity is God calling you today? Now?

112. *Inspirations are so many voices of God and share his power.*

When I was a seminarian, one day about thirty of us, priests and seminarians, were in the dining room. The phone rang. Whenever the phone rang during meals, someone needed to rise and answer. This time, I went to the phone and answered. A visiting Jesuit was with us at the moment, and the call was for him. I took the message and went to his room to deliver it.

After I gave him the message, we began to talk. The preceding summer, this priest had given the thirty-day Ignatian Spiritual Exercises to one of our seminarians. I had heard of this, and though I said nothing to anyone, a great desire stirred in me to do the same. Hesitantly, I asked the Jesuit if he would consider me for the retreat the coming summer. After we had spoken for a time, to my delight he said "yes." The next July, I made the thirty-day retreat under his guidance, and it has shaped much in my life since.

I was the first of our seminarians to study at the Pontifical Gregorian University in Rome. At one point, the priest in charge of our formation wanted to invite a professor, Father Manuel Ruiz Jurado, S.J., to give us a day of retreat. Father Ruiz Jurado is one of the leading experts on the Spiritual Exercises and Ignatian spirituality. Because I had him as a professor, our priest asked that I drive him from and back to the university.

On the drive back, Father Ruiz Jurado told me that he had leafed through a book of Venerable Bruno's writings he had found on the desk of his room. Among these was Venerable Bruno's *Directory* on how to give the Spiritual Exercises. Father Ruiz Jurado commented that this *Directory* would be an excellent topic for a licentiate thesis. The remark stayed in my mind, and when the time came to write a thesis, I asked Father Ruiz Jurado to be my moderator. He accepted, and I wrote my thesis on Venerable Bruno's *Directory*. This led later to a doctoral thesis, again with Father Ruiz Jurado as moderator. These studies proved key to my entire understanding of Venerable Bruno.

A few years after ordination, when I was stationed in Boston, one Thursday I got a call from the priest in charge of our downtown chapel. The priest who regularly said the 1:00 p.m. Sunday Mass in Spanish had had to return suddenly to his country, and now, at the last minute, there was no one to say the Mass. Our priest asked if I would be willing to say it. I had never celebrated Mass in Spanish, but answered that, in the circumstances, I would do my best.

I found a priest who was willing to translate my homily for me. I wrote it in English and took it to his rectory. I can still see him sitting at his desk, typing the text in Spanish. I memorized it, practiced the Mass in Spanish as well as I could, and did my best that Sunday.

It was the beginning of five years of intense Hispanic ministry that opened a new world for me. Several trips to Latin America followed, and I developed a grasp of Spanish that proved invaluable in my later research on discernment.

What if I had not answered the phone that day? What if I had not remembered and acted on Father Ruiz Jurado's words as we drove back to the university? What if I had declined when asked to say that Mass in Spanish?

"Inspirations are so many voices of God and share his power." Venerable Bruno is right. I wish that I always grasped and responded to God's inspirations!

The Holy Spirit, dwelling in us (1 Cor. 6:19), never ceases to work within us, inspiring, showing the way, opening the next door. "Listen, that you may have life" (Isa. 55:3).

113. *Above all, I have asked the Lord to give you great courage and firm hope in God, so that by this virtue, overcoming all discouragement and striving not to lose that precious time the Lord gives us, you may attain greater good for yourself and for others, especially since the Lord has given you so many means for this and the desire to accomplish it.*

"Above all, I have asked the Lord to give you great courage and firm hope in God." Ask, above all, for "great courage and firm hope in God" so that discouragement may never hold sway in you, and that you be free to employ "that precious time the Lord gives" for the greater good, for God's greater glory, to make him more known and loved.

Can you take a moment now and ask the Lord for "great courage and firm hope" so that the time given to you may bear ever greater fruit for God, "especially since the Lord has given you so many means for this and the desire to accomplish it"?

114. *I felt a desire to know him, to love him, to serve him as perfectly as I can, and to make him known, loved, and served by all. I no longer want any limits in my love for Jesus and for my neighbor.*

These words are found in personal retreat notes written after meditating on the love of Jesus Christ. We touch, here, the heart of Venerable Bruno's entire life.

"I felt a desire to know him." When I was in high school, my pastor, Father James Wolfe, gave me a copy of *To Know Christ Jesus* by Frank Sheed. It was a new kind of reading for me, and it helped me understand Jesus in a new way. I had not known that one could delve into Scripture in this manner and learn of Jesus so richly. It was the best book Father could have given me. Yes, this is the heart of our lives: to know Jesus. "Now this is eternal life, that they should know you, the only true God, and the one whom you sent, Jesus Christ" (John 17:3). This is "the supreme good of knowing Christ Jesus my Lord" (Phil. 3:8) for which St. Paul gives everything.

"I felt a desire ... to love him." "O God, you are my God—it is you I seek! ... Your love is better than life" (Ps. 63:2, 4). St. Thérèse: "And now I have no other desire than to love Jesus unto folly" (*The Story of a Soul*, VIII). Oblate Father Antonio Ferrero writes of Venerable Bruno's final illness, "Not content with sacramental Communion alone, he never ceased making spiritual communions, and his most frequent prayer was, *Jesu bone, sitio te* [Good Jesus, I thirst for you], or more briefly, with his eyes fixed on the tabernacle, *Sitio, sitio* [I thirst, I thirst]." The desire, the thirst, to love Jesus was the center of Venerable Bruno's life.

"I felt a desire ... to serve him as perfectly as I can." In his spiritual program, the young Bruno plans how he will live the first moments of the day: "Immediately upon awaking. My God and my all. I desire this day to please God and to fulfill his will in everything, and to do all for his greater glory." St. Ignatius of Loyola writes that "man is created to praise, reverence, and serve God our Lord, and by this means to save his soul." Venerable Bruno prayed this text many times, internalized it deeply, and desired to live it daily. His heart's desire was to serve Jesus, and to do this as best he could.

"I felt a desire ... to make him known, loved, and served by all." God is glorified when human hearts come to know him and to love him, in this life and unto eternity. God's greater glory is served by what causes more human hearts to know him, to love him, and so to enter eternal life. Venerable Bruno, as he prays, feels the desire to be God's instrument for this greater good, to make Jesus known, loved, and served by *all people*.

"I no longer want any limits in my love for Jesus and for my neighbor." *I no longer want limits.* Venerable Bruno wrote these words to describe a grace received in prayer. *No longer any limits.* Can we at least desire to say this to Jesus, to tell him that we no longer want limits in our love for him and for those he has given to us?

A FINAL WORD

Some time ago, I gathered with fifty people in the Benedictine Abbey in Schuyler, Nebraska. Most were laypeople; a few were religious or priests. Three of my fellow Oblates of the Virgin Mary were also present. We were gathered to share the spiritual teaching of Venerable Bruno.

Each morning and afternoon, for four days, I spoke on various themes in his teaching. This book originated from those days, as I watched the impact of Venerable Bruno's teaching upon the group. I saw doubts lifted, energy released, clarity received, hope instilled, and a joyful sense of new spiritual life pervade the group. I wanted to share that experience with others. With some additions and with further commentary, this book presents the quotations from Venerable Bruno that we explored in that retreat.

When we had finished, one person commented on "the hopefulness and the encouragement to be gentle with ourselves when we fail. The wonderful idea of always beginning again." Another said, "It was so practical and gave me a plan to grow in my spiritual life so that when the temptations come, I will be ready to be strong. It was encouraging even though I am weak." Yet another remarked, "I learned from Venerable Bruno how to build a spiritual program for my life."

OVERCOMING SPIRITUAL DISCOURAGEMENT

One participant said, "The content was life-changing." It is. It can be for you as well.

May Venerable Bruno be for you, too, a source of consolation and hope on the spiritual journey.

PRAYER FOR THE INTERCESSION
OF VENERABLE BRUNO

O Father, fountain of all life and holiness,
You gave Venerable Bruno Lanteri great faith in
    Christ, your Son, a lively hope, and an active
    love for the salvation of his brethren.
You made him a prophet of your word and a wit-
    ness to your mercy.
He had a tender love for Mary, and by his very
    life he taught fidelity to the Church.
Father, hear the prayer of your family, and,
    through the intercession of Venerable Bruno,
    grant us the grace for which we now ask …
May he be raised to the altars that we may give
    you greater praise. We ask this through your
    Son, Jesus Christ, our Lord. Amen.

★ ★ ★

To request prayers or share graces received through Venerable Bruno's intercession, and for information regarding
his cause of canonization, go to: https://www.omvusa.org/
bruno-lanteri/.

RESOURCES

Printed Resources

Timothy M. Gallagher, O.M.V., *Begin Again: The Life and Spiritual Legacy of Bruno Lanteri*, Crossroad, 2013.

Timothy M. Gallagher, ed., *The Venerable Bruno Lanteri: Spiritual Counsels for Life in the World*, Discerning Hearts, 2016.

Further print materials such as prayer cards, brochures, and prayer booklets are also available. For more information, visit the Venerable Bruno Lanteri website (https://www.omvusa.org/bruno-lanteri/) or email the Oblates at office@omvusa.org.

Digital Resources

Venerable Bruno Lanteri website:
www.omvusa.org/bruno-lanteri/.

Documentary film on Venerable Bruno, *Nunc Coepi*:
https://www.omvusa.org/bruno-lanteri/life-legacy/documentary/
view-documentary/ (English, Spanish, and Italian)

OVERCOMING SPIRITUAL DISCOURAGEMENT

For those interested in discerning a vocation to the Oblates of the Virgin Mary:

Vocation Director
Our Lady of Grace Seminary
1105 Boylston St., Boston, MA 02215
617.869.2429
vocations@omvusa.org
www.omvusa.org

SOURCES

Abbreviations

B Timothy M. Gallagher, O.M.V., *Begin Again: The Life and Spiritual Legacy of Bruno Lanteri*, New York: Crossroad, 2013.

C Paolo Calliari, O.M.V., ed., *Carteggio del Venerabile Padre Pio Bruno Lanteri (1759–1830) fondatore della Congregazione degli Oblati di Maria Vergine*, 5 vols., Turin: Editrice Lanteriana, 1976.

E Timothy M. Gallagher, O.M.V., ed., *Un'esperienza dello Spirito. Pio Bruno Lanteri: Il suo carisma nelle sue parole*, Cuneo: AGA, 1989.

G Pietro Gastaldi, O.M.V., *Della vita del Servo di Dio Pio Brunone Lanteri, fondatore della Congregazione degli Oblati di Maria Vergine*, Turin: Marietti, 1870.

P Amato Frutaz, ed., *Pinerolien. Beatificationis et canonizationis Servi Dei Pii Brunonis Lanteri fundatoris Congregationis Oblatorum M. V. (1830): Positio super introductione causae et super virtutibus ex officio compilata*, Rome: Typis Polyglottis Vaticanis, 1945.

S   Scritti e documenti d'archivio, Rome: Edizioni Lanteri,
    2002.

SC Timothy M. Gallagher, O.M.V., ed., *The Venerable Bruno
    Lanteri: Spiritual Counsels for Life in the World*, Omaha:
    Discerning Hearts, 2016.

Source of Each Quotation

1. B, 98–99.
2. B, 133–134.
3. B, 134.
4. E, 249.
5. B, 77.
6. B, 62.
7. B, 87–88.
8. B, 63.
9. P, 632.
10. S, 570.
11. B, 62.
12. C, 2, 323.
13. C, 2, 324.
14. C, 2, 324.
15. S, 1, 747.
16. S, 1, 748.
17. S, 1, 751.
18. S, 1, 752.
19. S, 1, 752.
20. S, 1, 757.
21. S I, 759–760.
22. S, 1, 760.
23. S 1, 571.
24. G, 170.
25. C, 2, 161.
26. SC, 35.
27. SC, 35.
28. SC, 35.
29. SC, 35.
30. SC, 35.
31. SC, 35.
32. SC, 568–569.
33. S, 1, 569.
34. S, 1, 569.
35. S, 1, 569.
36. S, 1, 569.
37. S, 1, 569.
38. S, 1, 569.
39. S, 1, 569.
40. S, 1, 569.
41. S, 1, 569.
42. S, 1, 569.
43. S, 1, 569.
44. S, 1, 569.
45. S, 1, 569.
46. C, 2, 344.
47. C, 2, 352.
48. SC, 7.

49. P, 536.
50. SC, 12.
51. S, 1, 558.
52. SC, 13–14.
53. S, 1, 562.
54. S, 1, 566.
55. B, 218.
56. C, 2, 168.
57. P, 537.
58. S, 1, 570.
59. SC, 38.
60. E, 126–127.
61. E, 127.
62. E, 127.
63. E, 127.
64. E, 127.
65. E, 127.
66. E, 148.
67. SC, 26.
68. C, 2, 314.
69. B, 73.
70. B, 75.
71. B, 22.
72. C, 2, 166.
73. C, 2, 314.
74. C, 2, 325.
75. C, 2, 352.
76. B, 147.
77. SC, 24–25.
78. C, 2, 321.
79. B, 49.
80. B, 49–50.
81. SC, 41.
82. SC, 41.
83. SC, 41.
84. SC, 41–42.
85. SC, 42.
86. B, 122.
87. B, 122.
88. B, 191.
89. B, 227.
90. B, 220.
91. B, 220.
92. B, 220.
93. B, 220.
94. B, 220.
95. B, 220.
96. B, 220.
97. B, 30.
98. S, 1, 563–564.
99. B, 62–63.
100. S, 1, 757.
101. S, 1, 757.
102. S, 1, 559.
103. S, 1, 559.
104. S, 1, 759.
105. C, 2, 306.
106. C, 2, 306–307.
107. C, 2, 307.
108. S, 1, 561.
109. S, 1, 560.
110. S, 1, 561.
111. S, 1, 561.
112. S, 1, 561.
113. C, 2, 251.
114. B, 34.

ABOUT THE AUTHOR

Father Timothy M. Gallagher, O.M.V., was ordained in 1979 as a member of the Oblates of the Virgin Mary, a religious community dedicated to giving retreats and spiritual formation according to the Spiritual Exercises of Saint Ignatius. Having obtained his doctorate in 1983 from the Gregorian University, he has taught (St. John's Seminary, Brighton, Massachusetts; Our Lady of Grace Seminary Residence, Boston), assisted in formation work, and served two terms as provincial in his community. He is a frequent speaker on EWTN, and his digitally recorded talks are used around the world. He has written ten books on Ignatian discernment and prayer, and several books on Venerable Bruno Lanteri and the Liturgy of the Hours. He currently holds the Saint Ignatius Chair for Spiritual Formation at Saint John Vianney Theological Seminary in Denver.